Quiz 2 Level 1

Questions	Answers
1 Are all snakes poisonous?	*No*
2 What is an iceberg?	*A large block of ice that floats in the sea*
3 What is *in the nick of time*?	*At the last possible moment*
4 Which came first, the Stone Age or the Bronze Age?	*The Stone Age*
5 What is the world's biggest ocean?	*The Pacific*
6 Who were the first people in Australia?	*The Aborigines*
7 Which black and white striped animal looks like the horse?	*The zebra*
8 What do we call the U–shaped plate nailed to a horse's hoof?	*A horseshoe*
9 Does the Earth travel round the Sun?	*Yes (once a year)*
10 Which bear has a white coat?	*The polar bear*

Quiz 1
Question 2

Quiz 1
Question 8

Quiz 3 Level 1

Questions	Answers
1 How many hours are there in a day?	**24**
2 What is meant by the saying *look before you leap*?	*Think carefully before you act*
3 Which joint lets you bend your arm?	*Your elbow*
4 Which precious stone is red?	*The ruby*
5 Which bird pecks holes in trees?	*The woodpecker*
6 What is the capital of the United Kingdom?	*London*
7 Who was the first woman prime minister of Great Britain?	*Margaret Thatcher*
8 What is the opposite of lazy?	*Hard-working*
9 Sneezy, Doc, Grumpy, Happy, Bashful, Dopey. Who else?	*Sleepy*
10 Does the Moon have any air?	*No. It has no wind or weather either*

Quiz 4
Question 3

Quiz 4
Question 7

FAMILY FLIP QUIZ

The questions are divided into six subjects: Natural World, History, Science and Maths, Geography, English, and General Knowledge. You should attempt all questions though.

There are four different levels of difficulty from level 1, the easiest, through to level 4, the most difficult.

KEY TO SYMBOLS

🌿	Natural World	🌍	Geography
🏛	History	📕	English
⚛	Science and Maths	❓	General Knowledge

Levels
There are three levels of question – they get harder as you progress

Question categories
The questions are divided into six subjects (see key above)

Picture clues 1
These visual clues are not always obvious (and they don't have labels)

This is how to use your *Family Flip Quiz*: if you are answering questions on your own just cover the answers with your hand or a piece of card. You may want to write down your answers and count up your scores for each quiz.

If you are doing the quizzes with a partner or in teams, unfold the base and stand *Family Flip Quiz* on a flat surface between you and your partner. Read aloud the questions (but not the answers!) and allow your partner to say the answers or write them down. You may answer each question in turn or answer an entire quiz in turn. Keep your scores on a piece of paper and compare results.

The illustrations are there to help you get the right answers when competing with a partner. For instance, if you are answering Quiz 1 questions, you will be looking at and reading out Quiz 2. However, the illustrations you will see are clues to help you do Quiz 1. Look at the labels by the illustrations. These tell you which question they are clues for. The pictures behind the quiz numbers at the top of the page are not such obvious clues, but they may still help you get the answer.

Quiz 112 Level 3

		Questions	Answers
1	🌿	Which Australian bird is also called the laughing jackass?	The kookaburra
2	❓	Which sport uses the smaller ball, tennis or squash?	Squash
3	❓	What is the name of the famous statue of the goddess Venus in the Louvre Museum in Paris?	Venus de Milo
4	🏛	Gandhi was given the name Mahatma. What does *Mahatma* mean?	Great soul
5	📕	What is an ampersand?	The character &
6	🌿	What is ebony?	A hard jet-black wood
7	❓	Which method of healing involves inserting needles into the body at certain points?	Acupuncture
8	📕	*They jumped through the hoop.* Which is the verb in that sentence?	Jumped
9	⚛	Which planet is called the Ringed Planet?	Saturn
10	🏛	What did William Wallace and Robert the Bruce fight for about 700 years ago?	Scotland's independence
11	🌿	Which is the only creature that can turn its head in an almost complete circle?	The owl
12	🏛	For which service did press gangs recruit men in the early 19th century?	The navy
13	⚛	What is the name of the disorder caused by pollen from plants floating in the air?	Hayfever
14	❓	What does NASA, in the USA do?	Launches spacecraft and satellites
15	📕	What won't a rolling stone gather?	Moss

Quiz 35
Question 11

Quiz 35
Question 6

Picture clues 2
These visual clues will often help you get the answer – the label tells you which question they refer to

Answers
When doing the quizzes on your own, cover the answers with your hand or a piece of card

Quiz 1 Level 1

Questions	Answers
1 What are the Himalayas, the Alps and Pyrenees examples of?	*Mountain ranges*
2 Which is the biggest land animal?	*The African elephant*
3 What is the opposite of *above*?	*Below*
4 Where is the Antarctic?	*At the South Pole*
5 Is the Sun a star?	*Yes*
6 Who was Cleopatra?	*The last queen of Egypt*
7 What does *to lose your nerve* mean?	*To become afraid*
8 What is an igloo?	*An Inuit house built of ice blocks*
9 In which American city would you find Central Park?	*New York*
10 What shape has three sides?	*A triangle*

Quiz 2
Question 10

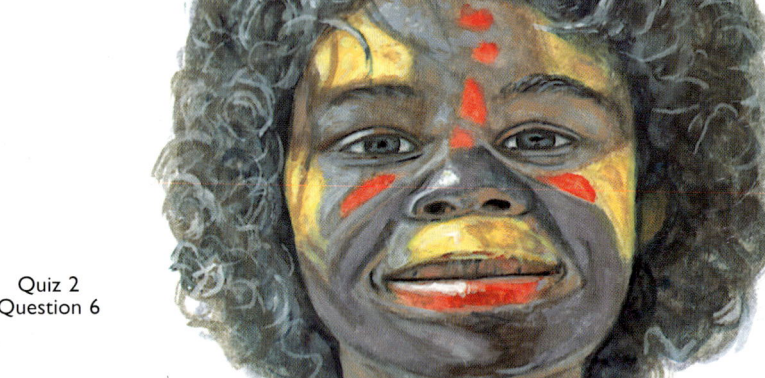

Quiz 2
Question 6

Quiz 4 Level 1

Questions	Answers

1	Who was the German leader during World War II?	*Adolf Hitler*
2	Which is the world's highest mountain?	*Mount Everest 8,848 m (29,028 ft)*
3	Which is the largest bird?	*The ostrich*
4	What is the capital of France?	*Paris*
5	What is meant by the saying *many hands make light work*?	*If a task is shared by many, it is easier*
6	Where are your taste buds?	*On your tongue*
7	Heads of United States presidents are carved into which mountain?	*Mount Rushmore*
8	Which saint is Santa Claus called after?	*St Nicholas*
9	What is the rough outside of a tree called?	*The bark*
10	What was Cinderella's coach made from?	*A pumpkin*

Quiz 3
Question 7

Quiz 3
Question 5

Quiz 5 Level 1

Questions

Answers

		Questions	Answers
1		What grows in paddy fields?	*Rice*
2		Which children's story tells of a wooden puppet that comes to life?	*'Pinocchio'*
3		Where is the Eiffel Tower?	*Paris, France*
4		Who won the race between the hare and the tortoise?	*The tortoise*
5		Which filmstar wore a bowler hat and carried a cane in his films?	*Charlie Chaplin*
6		Which ancient people first built pyramids?	*The Egyptians*
7		Where does gold come from?	*Out of the earth, or as grains in streams*
8		What is the main ingredient of ketchup?	*Tomato*
9		What is the next number in this sequence: 4·5, 5, 5·5, 6?	*6·5*
10		Which animal is *king of the beasts*?	*The lion*

Quiz 6
Question 5

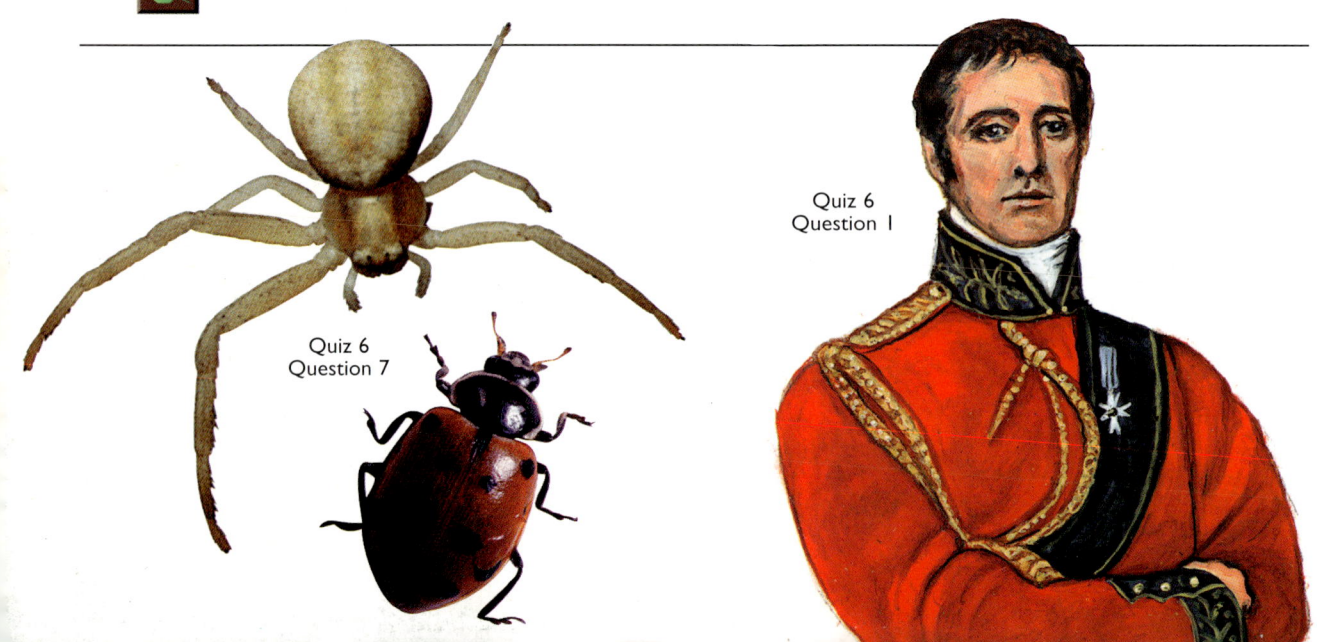

Quiz 6
Question 7

Quiz 6
Question 1

Quiz 6 Level 1

Questions

Answers

1. Which famous general gave his name to the Wellington boot? — *The Duke of Wellington*

2. What is a Tam o' Shanter? — *A flat-topped cap*

3. Where is Mount Snowdon? — *Wales*

4. Complete this saying: *As dry as a...* — *Bone*

5. What does a caterpillar turn into? — *A butterfly or a moth*

6. Which sport is associated with Wimbledon? — *Tennis*

7. Is a spider an insect? — *No (insects have 6 legs, spiders have 8)*

Quiz 5
Question 8

8. Do camels store water in their humps? — *No (their humps are full of fat)*

9. Which parts of the Earth have the longest summer days? — *The North and South Poles*

10. What do we use our lungs for? — *Breathing*

Quiz 5
Question 2

Quiz 5
Question 10

Quiz 7 Level 1

	Questions	Answers
1	What is the opposite of soft?	*Hard*
2	In which sea does the island of Malta lie?	*The Mediterranean Sea*
3	What country did Pelé play for?	*Brazil*
4	Which girl walked along the Yellow Brick Road?	*Dorothy in 'The Wizard of Oz'*
5	Where does a mole live?	*Under the ground*
6	Which is the Earth's only natural satellite?	*The Moon*
7	What is the capital of Russia?	*Moscow*
8	Which bear did A.A. Milne write about?	*Winnie the Pooh*
9	What is a young cow called?	*A calf*
10	Do all birds fly?	*No. Penguins, kiwis and ostriches do not*

Quiz 8
Question 6

Quiz 8
Question 1

Quiz 8 Level 1

Questions	Answers
1 Which country does spaghetti come from?	*Italy*
2 In which country does the emu live?	*Australia*
3 What frightened Miss Muffet away?	*A spider*
4 What are car tyres made of?	*Rubber*
5 What was Cinderella's slipper made of?	*Glass*
6 Which bird is the symbol of peace?	*The dove*
7 What are cappuccino and espresso?	*Coffee drinks*
8 What was the Spanish Armada?	*A fleet of ships sent to fight England*
9 What is a young horse called?	*A foal*
10 What is the stern of a ship?	*The back*

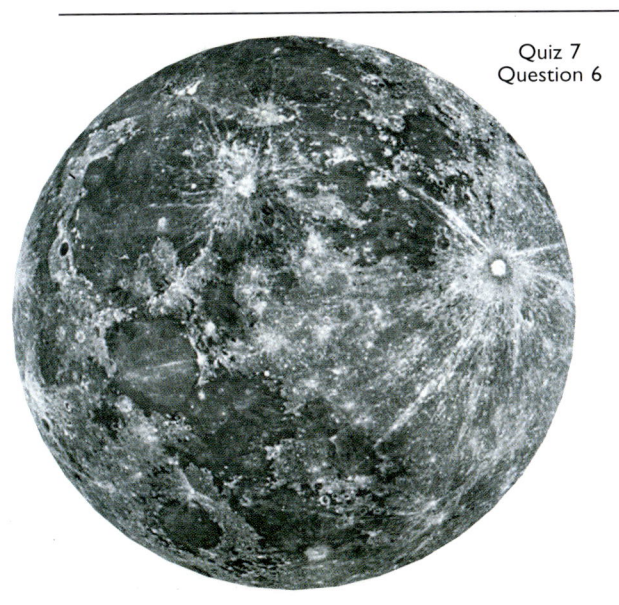

Quiz 7
Question 6

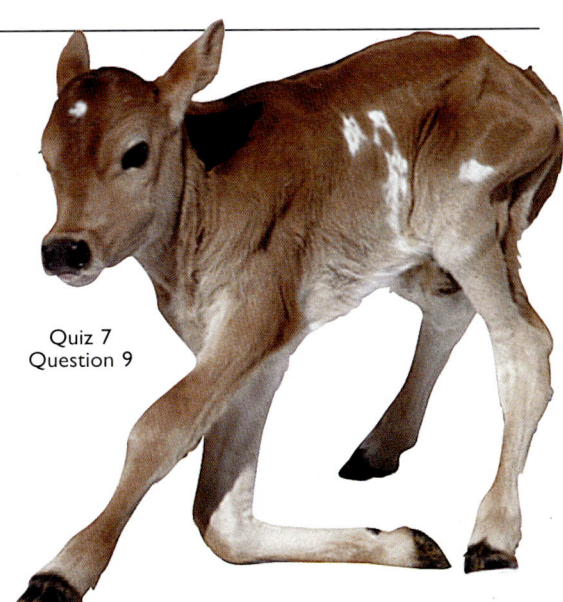

Quiz 7
Question 9

Quiz 9 Level 1

Questions

Answers

		Question	Answer
1		What is made from chocolate at Easter?	*Easter eggs and Easter bunnies*
2		What sort of creature was a Diplodocus?	*A dinosaur*
3		Who was the religious member of Robin Hood's band?	*Friar Tuck*
4		Who wrote *The Ugly Duckling*?	*Hans Christian Andersen*
5		What is caught in pots in the sea?	*Lobsters and crabs*
6		Which is the smallest breed of dog?	*The chihuahua*
7		Which country names its years after animals?	*China*
8		How often is the football world cup played?	*Every 4 years*
9		At which battle in 1314 did Robert Bruce defeat the English?	*The Battle of Bannockburn*
10		What is 21 + 0?	*21*

Quiz 10
Question 1

Quiz 10
Question 4

Quiz 10 Level 1

Questions

1. Who did Simple Simon meet on his way to the fair?

2. What is a hurricane?

3. How many sides does a hexagon have?

4. What are young ducks called?

5. Who wrote *Charlie and the Chocolate Factory*?

6. Are any two fingerprints the same?

7. What is insomnia?

8. Around which sea was the Roman empire?

9. What is the Muslim holy book called?

10. What makes your pulse beat?

Answers

A pieman

A storm with very strong winds

6

Ducklings

Roald Dahl

No, not even those of identical twins

An inability to sleep

The Mediterranean Sea

The Koran

Your heart pumping blood

Quiz 9 Question 6

Quiz 9 Question 3

Quiz 9 Question 5

Quiz 11 Level 1

Questions	Answers
1 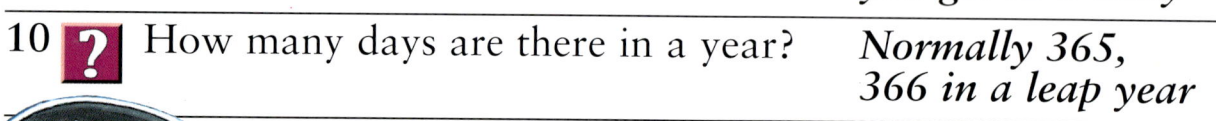 Which is the world's biggest desert?	*The Sahara in Africa*
2 What are the Wright brothers famous for?	*They flew the first powered aircraft*
3 Shot put, pole vault and javelin are examples of what?	*Athletic sports*
4 Who said: *Elementary my dear Watson?*	*Sherlock Holmes*
5 What is the ingredient that makes bread rise?	*Yeast*
6 What colour was the owl and the pussycat's boat?	*Pea green*
7 Which ancient civilization grew up around the river Nile?	*The Egyptian civilization*
8 Which vegetable has a big orange-red root?	*The carrot*
9 What are your milk teeth?	*The first set of teeth you get as a baby*
10 How many days are there in a year?	*Normally 365, 366 in a leap year*

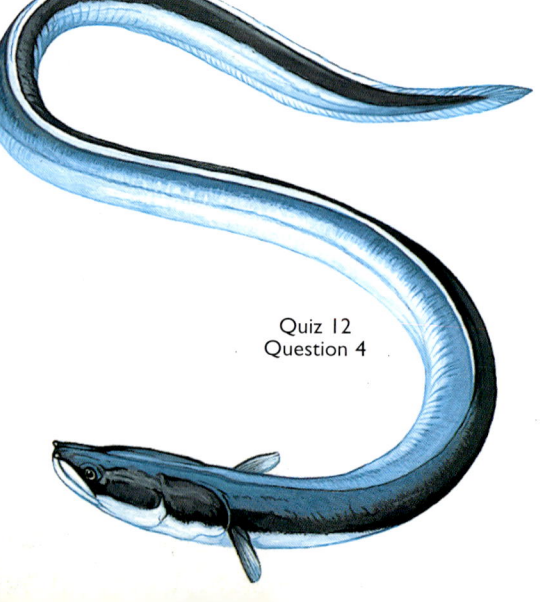

Quiz 12
Question 4

Quiz 12
Question 2

Quiz 12 Level 1

Questions	Answers
1 Where is the kimono worn?	*In Japan*
2 Which ancient king had a round table?	*King Arthur*
3 In which town was Jesus born?	*Bethlehem*
4 Which fish looks like a snake?	*An eel*
5 What is a female fox called?	*A vixen*
6 What is the London home of the Royal family?	*Buckingham Palace*
7 What is 54 – 0?	*54*
8 Which is the biggest city in Scotland?	*Glasgow*
9 What does an elephant use for smelling and lifting things?	*Its trunk*
10 What is the plural of roof?	*Roofs*

Quiz 11
Question 8

Quiz 11
Question 6

Quiz 11
Question 4

Quiz 13 Level 1

Questions	Answers
1 What is cutlery?	*Knives, forks and spoons*
2 When we serve a drink *on the rocks* what do we mean?	*It is served with ice*
3 Which sub-group of animals do mice, rats and squirrels belong to?	*Rodents*
4 Are there mountains under the ocean?	*Yes*
5 Who spent three days inside a whale?	*Jonah*
6 Does wood float?	*Yes*
7 What are tributaries?	*Streams feeding into a large river*
8 What did Alexander Graham Bell invent in 1876?	*The telephone*
9 What is a young bear called?	*A cub*
10 How many people are on the field during a football game?	*23 (2 teams and a referee)*

Quiz 14
Question 5

Quiz 14
Question 1

Quiz 14
Question 3

Quiz 14 Level 1

Questions

Answers

1. What cathedral in the City of London has a Whispering Gallery? — *St Paul's Cathedral*

2. What is the capital of Greece? — *Athens*

3. Which rabbit-like animal has long ears and long back legs? — *The hare*

4. Do lines of latitude run north and south or east and west? — *East and west*

5. In *The Wizard of Oz*, which character was looking for a heart? — *The Tin Man*

6. Which mountain did Edmund Hillary climb in 1953? — *Mount Everest*

7. What keeps a hovercraft up? — *A cushion of air*

8. In which sport do people use pommel horses and parallel bars? — *Gymnastics*

9. What is the word *flu* short for? — *Influenza*

10. How does the kangaroo move along at speed? — *By taking large leaps*

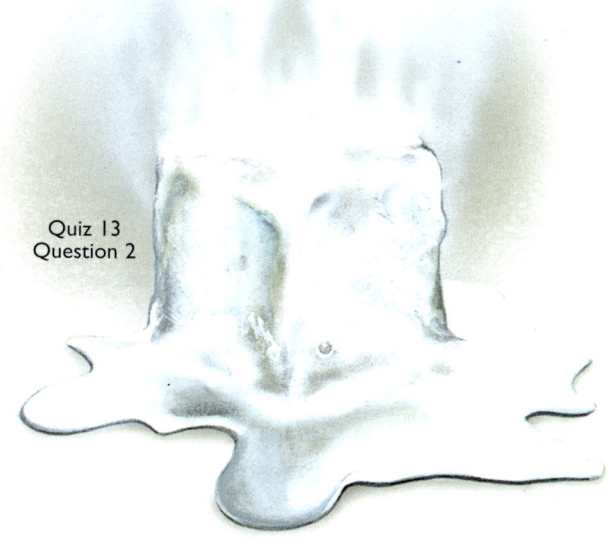

Quiz 13
Question 2

Quiz 13
Question 8

Quiz 15 Level 1

Questions	Answers
1 How many cards are in a pack?	52
2 What form of transport does a cavalry regiment use?	Horses
3 Where does the Pope live?	In Vatican City
4 Which snake makes a noise with its tail?	The rattlesnake
5 Which canal links the Red Sea with the Mediterranean?	The Suez Canal
6 Where did little Jack Horner sit?	In the corner
7 You can see through it and it's made from sand. What is it?	Glass
8 Which creature has a sting in its tail?	The scorpion
9 Who was the Maid of Orléans?	Joan of Arc
10 What does a stitch in time save?	9 (stitches)

Quiz 16
Question 6

Quiz 16
Question 3

Quiz 16 Level 1

Questions

Answers

1	What does *keep your nose clean* mean?	*Keep out of trouble*
2	Which part of the body do you use for hearing and balancing?	*Your ears*
3	According to the Christmas carol, which bird is in the pear tree?	*A partridge*
4	Where is the Statue of Liberty?	*On an island in New York harbour*
5	What was a legionary?	*A Roman soldier*
6	Which animal do they herd in Lapland?	*The reindeer*
7	Which girl's grandmother was eaten by a wolf?	*Little Red Riding Hood*
8	Who created Mickey Mouse and Donald Duck?	*Walt Disney*
9	What shape is a sphere?	*Ball-shaped*
10	What is 5½ as a decimal?	*5.5*

Quiz 15
Question 9

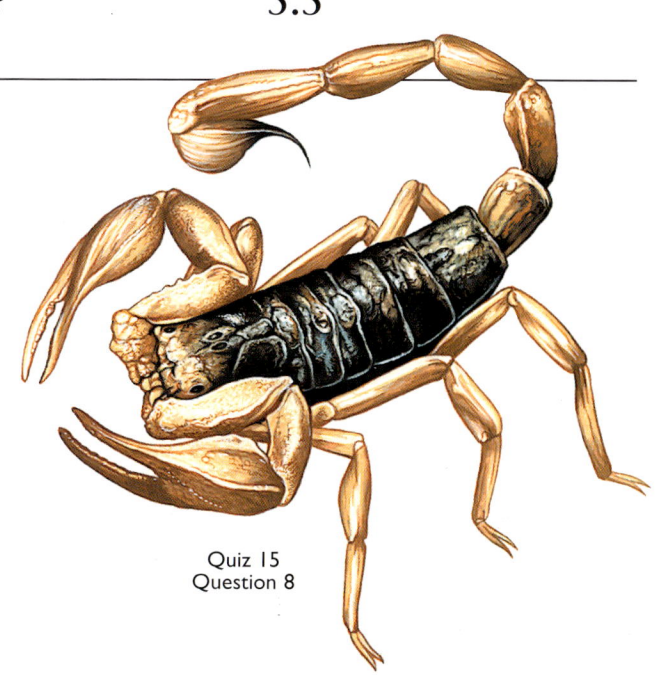

Quiz 15
Question 8

Quiz 17 Level 1

Questions	Answers
1 What is a noun?	A person, place or thing
2 Which brass instrument has a sliding section?	The trombone
3 What is the capital of Northern Ireland?	Belfast
4 What is created when a meteorite hits a planet?	A crater
5 What do we do when we have a nap?	Have a short sleep
6 What did David use to kill Goliath?	A stone in a sling
7 Why do you sneeze?	To clear something from your nose
8 Which was the biggest dinosaur?	Brachiosaurus
9 Which bird has big, round eyes at the front of its head?	The owl
10 What is another name for the Netherlands?	Holland

Quiz 18
Question 1

Quiz 18
Question 8

Quiz 18 Level 1

	Questions	Answers
1	Which flower commemorates the war dead?	*The poppy*
2	What is another word for *begin*?	*Start or commence*
3	How many bones are in the human body?	*206*
4	Which rugby team is called the All-Blacks?	*The New Zealand team*
5	Who built the Sphinx?	*The ancient Egyptians*
6	What are Scottish lakes called?	*Lochs*
7	What is irrigation?	*The supply of water for crops*
8	Who wrote *Twelfth Night*, *Hamlet*, and *Macbeth*?	*William Shakespeare*
9	Which book told the adventures of Toad of Toad Hall?	*'Wind in the Willows'*
10	Where is the Amazon rainforest?	*In South America (mainly in Brazil)*

Quiz 17
Question 7

Quiz 17
Question 9

Quiz 19 Level 1

Questions	Answers
1 Which island is at the toe of Italy?	Sicily
2 Who are the infantry?	Soldiers who fight on foot
3 The Chinese were making ice cream some 5,000 years ago. True or false?	True
4 Which people wrote in hieroglyphics?	The ancient Egyptians
5 Which creature did St George slay?	A dragon
6 What is the capital of Germany?	Berlin
7 What is another word for *unite*?	Join
8 Is alcohol a drug?	Yes
9 What is a cylinder?	It is a tube shaped like a can of beans
10 What is kelp?	Seaweed

Quiz 20
Question 6

Quiz 20
Question 1

Quiz 20 Level 1

Questions	Answers
1 Punch and Judy are what?	*Puppets*
2 Who lived in Sherwood Forest?	*Robin Hood*
3 Which American animal sprays out a foul-smelling fluid to defend itself?	*The skunk*
4 Who was the first black president of South Africa?	*Nelson Mandela*
5 If I have 36 bananas, how many people can I give three to?	*12 people*
6 Which garden pest is related to the snail?	*The slug*
7 Who was Winnie the Pooh's donkey friend?	*Eeyore*
8 What is the Indy 500?	*A motor-racing event*
9 On which British coin can you see a portcullis?	*On the penny*
10 What happens to your eyes when you sneeze?	*They close*

Quiz 19
Question 5

Quiz 19
Question 3

Quiz 21 Level 1

Questions

Answers

1 Which game is played in a four-walled court with a small rubber ball? — *Squash*

2 In which country was tea first grown? — *China*

Quiz 22
Question 5

3 Which is the fastest passenger aircraft? — *Supersonic Concorde*

4 Which is the wealthiest nation? — *The USA*

5 What is the shape of one side of a cube? — *A square*

6 Who led Britain through World War II? — *Winston Churchill*

7 How often are the Olympic Games held? — *Every 4 years*

8 What is another word for *suspend*? — *Hang*

9 Which animal is said to have nine lives? — *The cat*

10 What is the name for the imaginary line around the middle of the Earth? — *The Equator*

Quiz 22
Question 9

Questions

Answers

		Questions	Answers
1		What is the masculine of goose?	*Gander*
2		Which country has a military force called the Foreign Legion?	*France*
3		What colours are the jerseys of the Newcastle United football team?	*Black and white vertical stripes*
4		Which sea does the river Nile flow into?	*The Mediterranean*
5		What is the national emblem of Wales?	*The leek*
6		What is the popular name for the Boeing 747?	*The Jumbo Jet*
7		Why is it dark at night?	*The Earth turns from the Sun*
8		A Triceratops was what?	*A dinosaur*
9		What was the bombing of London called during World War II?	*The Blitz*
10		Which is the tallest animal?	*The giraffe*

Quiz 21
Question 9

Quiz 21
Question 6

Quiz 23 Level 1

Questions

Answers

1. What is another word for *difficult*?

   Hard

2. Which forbidden fruit did Adam and Eve eat?

   The apple

3. What is the plural of mother-in-law?

   Mothers-in-law

4. How many sides has an octagon?

   8

5. Who is the heir apparent to Britain's throne?

   Prince Charles

6. Which plant contains nicotine?

   Tobacco plant

7. Which is the world's biggest animal?

   The Blue whale

8. What powers London's underground trains?

   Electricity

9. What was the *Luftwaffe*?

   The German air force

10. What is the Great Barrier Reef in Australia made of?

    Coral

Quiz 24
Question 7

Quiz 24
Question 5

Quiz 24 Level 1

Questions

1. What do *too many cooks* do?

2. What are back, breast, and crawl?

3. What were zeppelins?

4. What's behind your ribs?

5. Where are the Crown Jewels?

Quiz 23 Question 2

6. Which country is famous for canals, windmills and bulb fields?

7. How many sides does a cube have?

8. How many people play or sing in a quartet?

9. What sank the *SS Titanic*?

10. Where is Fujiyama?

Answers

Spoil the broth

Swimming strokes

Early German airships

Your lungs

In the Tower of London

Holland

6 square sides

4

An iceberg

In Japan

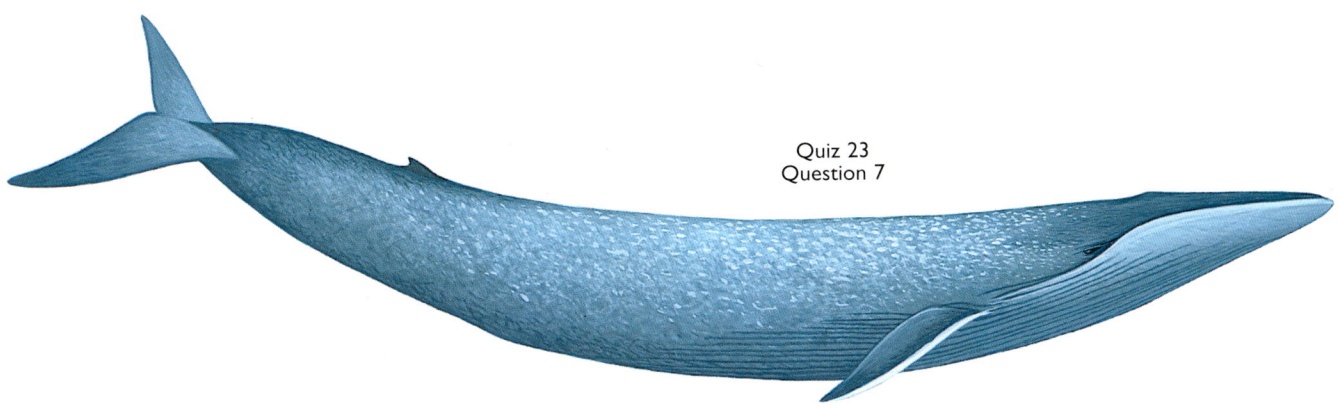

Quiz 23
Question 7

Quiz 25 Level 1

Questions

Answers

1. Which American president was assassinated in Dallas, Texas?

   John Kennedy

2. What is the usual number of kidneys humans have?

   2

3. What is the main language spoken in Turkey?

   Turkish

4. What are *Sleeping Beauty*, *Giselle*, and *Swan Lake*?

   Ballets

5. Which bridge in London can be lifted?

   Tower Bridge

6. Where is the pupil in your eye?

   In the centre of the coloured part

7. Tyrannosaurus was what?

   A flesh-eating dinosaur

8. Where did gladiators originally come from?

   Ancient Rome

9. What is *to pull the wool over someone's eyes*?

   To deceive someone

10. Which is the most common disease?

    The common cold

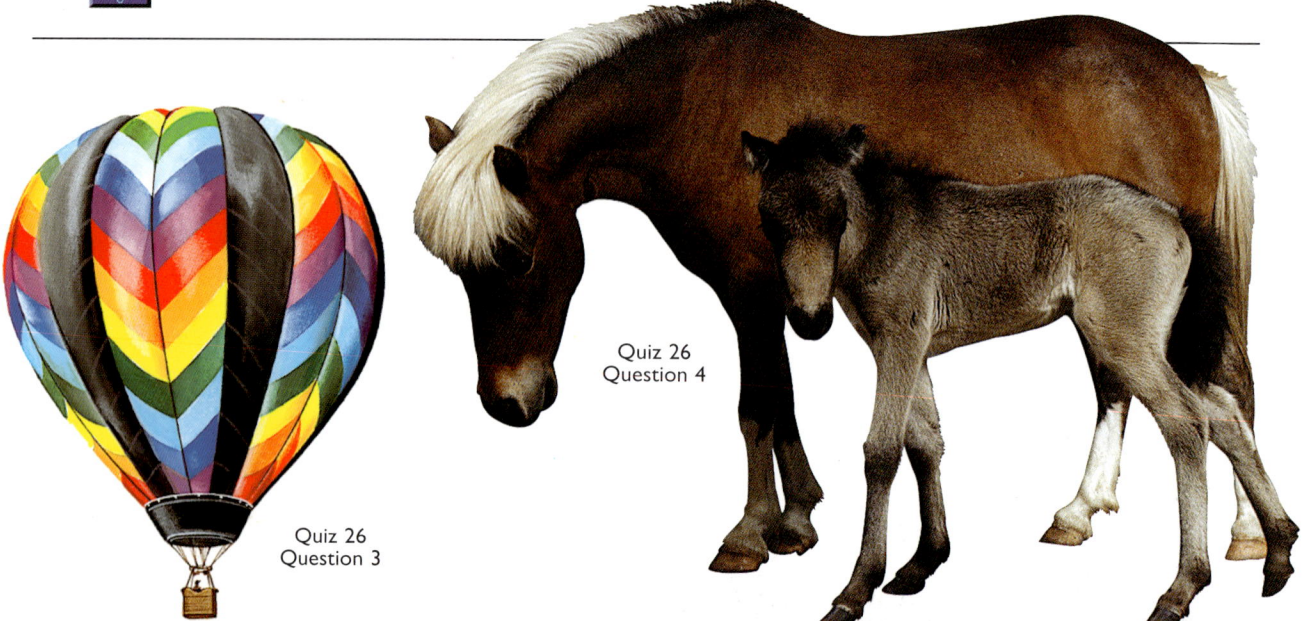

Quiz 26
Question 3

Quiz 26
Question 4

Quiz 26 Level 1

Questions	Answers
1 What couldn't Jack Sprat eat?	Fat
2 Which country do the Springboks represent?	South Africa
3 When does an air balloon rise?	When the air inside it is heated
4 Where is the mane of a horse?	Down the back of its neck
5 Why do some people *touch wood*?	To prevent bad luck
6 Where would you be likely to meet a Maori?	New Zealand
7 Cream, butter, cheese and yoghurt are all made from what?	Milk
8 Which city are Romulus and Remus supposed to have founded?	Rome
9 What is a half of a half?	A quarter
10 What makes up a galaxy?	Stars

Quiz 25
Question 1

Quiz 25
Question 8

Quiz 27 Level 1

Questions

Answers

1. What is the Italian currency?

   The lira

2. What are judo, karate, kendo, aikado, kung-fu examples of?

   Marshal arts

3. Where is it dark all day in winter?

   At the North and South Poles

4. Which animal does ham and pork come from?

   The pig

5. Children have faster pulse rates than adults. True or false?

   True

6. Who was messenger for the Roman gods?

   Mercury

7. Which country did Joseph Stalin rule?

   The Soviet Union (Russia)

8. What do we mean when we say *the pot is calling the kettle black*?

   You are criticizing others for faults

9. How many straight edges does a cube have?

   12

10. The Union and Confederate states fought in which war?

    The American Civil War

Quiz 28
Question 4

Quiz 28
Question 7

Quiz 28 Level 1

Questions

Answers

		Question	Answer
1		If you read 12 pages a day, how long will it take to read a 60-page book?	*5 days*
2		If the date is 1820, is it the 17th, 18th, or 19th century?	*19th century*
3		What is the currency of the USA?	*The dollar*
4		Which pear is not a pear?	*An avocado pear*
5		What are Labradors, Airedales and St Bernards?	*Breeds of dog*
6		Where are Notre Dame, Sacre Coeur, and the Eiffel Tower?	*In Paris*
7		What is the young of a goat called?	*A kid*
8		What were Spitfires and Hurricanes?	*RAF fighters in World War II*
9		Do you breathe in and out 5 times, 10 times, or 20 times each minute?	*About 20 times when you're resting*
10		Which is the first book of the Bible?	*Genesis*

Quiz 27
Question 6

Quiz 27
Question 4

Quiz 29 Level 1

Questions

Answers

		Questions	Answers
1		A river flows towards the sea. True or false?	*True*
2		How many grams are there in a kilogram?	*1,000*
3		What kind of fruit does a vine produce?	*Grapes*
4		What did the dish run away with?	*The spoon*
5		Which Indian leader lead his country in peaceful resistance?	*Mahatma Gandhi*
6		On a compass, which direction is 90 degrees anticlockwise of East?	*North*
7		If a king abdicates, what does he do?	*He gives up his throne*
8		Napoleon Bonaparte was a leader of which country?	*France*
9		Which sea lies between Africa and Europe?	*The Mediterranean*
10		What is lightning?	*An electrical discharge*

Quiz 30
Question 4

Quiz 30
Question 1

Quiz 30 Level 1

Questions

1. Which flying machine has a rotor and a propeller?

2. How can you tell if a shape is symmetrical?

3. Which is the odd one out: Asia, Australia, China, North America?

4. Which Australian marsupial looks like a bear?

5. What is the plural of *knife*?

6. Who killed Cock Robin?

7. What is a young deer called?

8. Where was William the Conqueror from?

9. In which country would you find the towns of Nice and Marseilles?

10. Which of these numbers are exactly divisible by 3: 6, 8, 12, 24?

Answers

A helicopter

One fold gives 2 identical halves

China (the others are continents)

The koala

Knives

The sparrow

A fawn

Normandy in France

France

6, 12, 24

Quiz 29
Question 5

Quiz 29
Question 6

Quiz 29
Question 4

Quiz 31 Level 1

Questions

Answers

		Questions	Answers
1		What work did the Seven Dwarfs do?	*They worked in a mine*
2		What is mutton?	*Meat from sheep over one year old*
3		Where is Bombay?	*India*
4		What colour are British fire engines?	*Red*
5		What emerged from Aladdin's lamp?	*A genie*
6		What are cirrus and cumulus examples of?	*Clouds*
7		What is chocolate made from?	*Cocoa beans*
8		What does temperature measure?	*Heat*
9		What is the modern name of the Roman port of *Londinium*?	*London*
10		How many metres are there in half a kilometre?	*500*

Quiz 32
Question 5

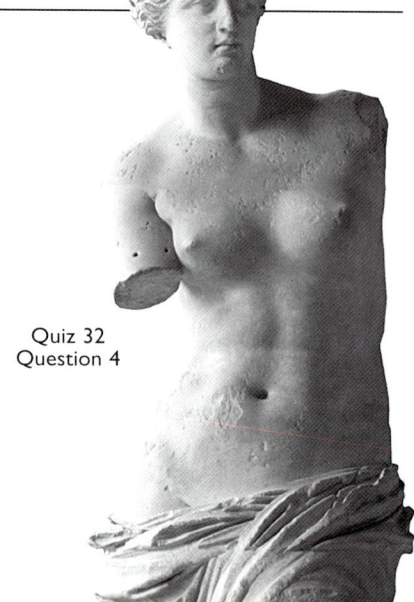

Quiz 32
Question 4

Quiz 32 Level 1

Questions | Answers

#	Question	Answer
1	What does Popeye eat for strength?	*Spinach*
2	Which part of an aeroplane is the fuselage?	*The body*
3	How many blackbirds were baked in the pie?	*24*
4	Which limbs of the *Venus de Milo* are missing?	*The arms*
5	Which animal is usually ridden in the desert?	*The camel*
6	Can you ride on African elephants?	*No, only on Indian elephants*
7	Which of these numbers can be divided by both 3 and 4: 9, 12, 15, 16?	*12*
8	In which English city was there a great fire in 1666?	*London*
9	A recipe needs 80 grams of butter, I have 55 grams. How much do I need?	*25 grams*
10	With which colour is Robin Hood associated?	*Green*

Quiz 31
Question 3

Quiz 31
Question 5

Quiz 33 Level 1

Questions

Answers

1. What are the uprights of cricket wickets called?
   Stumps

2. How many fiddlers had Old King Cole?
   3

3. Who wore a coat of many colours?
   Joseph

4. Iceberg and Cos are types of what?
   Lettuces

5. Where is the bow of a ship?
   At the front

6. Which bird lays the largest egg?
   The ostrich

7. Which is larger: 8 x 14 or 14 x 8?
   Neither. They both equal 112

8. What did Guy Fawkes try to blow up?
   The Houses of Parliament

9. What are Catherine Wheels and Roman Candles examples of?
   Fireworks

10. Where is Venice?
    Italy

Quiz 34
Question 7

Quiz 34
Question 9

Quiz 34 Level 1

Questions	Answers
1 What is the opposite of the word *brave*?	*Cowardly*
2 The date is 10th May. What will the date be in two weeks' time?	*24th May*
3 What does a greengrocer sell?	*Fruit and vegetables*
4 What is a quarter of a half?	*An eighth*
5 Which island lies just south of Hampshire?	*The Isle of Wight*
6 What is the plural of sheep?	*Sheep*
7 Frog spawn, tadpole. What comes next?	*Frog*
8 What is the name for a moving staircase?	*An escalator*
9 What were German submarines called?	*U-boats*
10 For which sport would you practise on nursery slopes?	*Skiing*

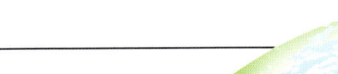

Quiz 33
Question 4

Quiz 33
Question 10

Quiz 35 Level 1

Questions

Answers

		Questions	Answers
1		Does air have weight?	*Yes*
2		What is the capital of the USA?	*Washington DC*
3		Which queen ruled Britain for 64 years?	*Queen Victoria*
4		How many 4s are there in 56?	*14*
5		If today is Tuesday, what was the day before yesterday?	*Sunday*
6		What word do we use for a book of maps?	*An atlas*
7		How many metres are there in 4.5 km?	*4,500*
8		Munich, Berlin and Hamburg are in which country?	*Germany*
9		Which of these animals is a carnivore: squirrel, leopard, rabbit, or giraffe?	*The leopard*
10		What is the opposite of generous?	*Mean or stingy*

Quiz 36
Question 7

Quiz 36 Level 1

Questions

Answers

		Question	Answer
1		In which country is the Costa del Sol?	*Spain*
2		In which game is a shuttlecock used?	*Badminton*
3		What is the plural of mouse?	*Mice*
4		In which century is 1314?	*14th*
5		Where is Ayers Rock?	*Australia*
6		What do you call a barrier that holds back water?	*A dam*
7		Which aircraft carries the most passengers?	*Jumbo jet*
8		Where are your incisors?	*In your mouth (they are teeth)*
9		How many wives did Henry VIII have?	*6*
10		What is the past tense of eat?	*Ate*

Quiz 35
Question 3

Quiz 35
Question 9

Quiz 37 Level 1

Questions

Answers

1. What currency is used in France?

   The franc

2. What tree does an acorn come from?

   The oak

3. What are forget-me-nots and marigolds examples of?

   Flowers

4. What is another name for a micro-processor in a computer?

   A microchip or a silicon chip

5. What is 7 less than 3,000?

   2,993

6. What is an ingot?

   A brick-shaped bar of gold

Quiz 38
Question 3

7. What did the dinosaur Stegosaurus have on its back?

   Large, upright plates

8. Which games held every 4 years first took place in ancient Greece?

   The Olympic Games

9. What are winkle-pickers – farmers, a type of shoe, a type of food?

   A type of shoe

10. Handel, Mozart and Brahms were all what?

    Composers

Quiz 38
Question 9

Quiz 38 Level 1

Questions

		Answers
1	What fleet of ships tried to invade England in 1588?	*The Spanish Armada*
2	What has the head and body of a woman and a long fish tail?	*A mermaid, according to legend*
3	The tubing of which brass wind instrument is curved into circles?	*The French horn*
4	In a desert, what is an area which has water called?	*An oasis*
5	What is a thatched roof made from?	*Straw or reed*
6	What shape is the base of a pyramid?	*A square*
7	Which country has the largest population?	*China*
8	In what sport are there scrums, line-outs and tries?	*Rugby*
9	Is an iguana a mammal, marsupial or reptile?	*A reptile*
10	What is a large group of lions called?	*A pride*

Quiz 37
Question 3

Quiz 37
Question 7

Quiz 39 Level 2

Questions

Answers

		Question	Answer
1		Are there any bees without stings?	*Yes*
2		What do we mean when we say someone is like *a cat on hot bricks*?	*The person is restless*
3		Which is the longest and narrowest country?	*Chile*
4		Which French leader was defeated at the battle of Waterloo?	*Napoleon Bonaparte*
5		Who was the last American president to be assassinated?	*John F. Kennedy (1963)*
6		Who sang the song *Yellow Submarine*?	*The Beatles*
7		Which animal lives on the seabed and has tentacles but looks like a flower?	*A sea anemone*
8		For how long does a baby grow inside its mother?	*Nine months*
9		What is an ellipse?	*A flattened circle*
10		What is an oasis?	*A fertile place in a desert*
11		What is a space probe?	*An unmanned spacecraft*
12		Cox and Golden Delicious are the names of what kind of fruit?	*The apple*
13		Which of these is not a reptile: tortoise, alligator, octopus, snake?	*Octopus*
14		What does the proverb *the pen is mightier than the sword* mean?	*Words are stronger than force*
15		What do 25, 16 and 9 have in common?	*They are all square numbers*

Quiz 40
Question 5

Quiz 40
Question 10

Quiz 40 Level 2

Questions

Answers

		Question	Answer
1		Is the Earth completely round?	*No. It is slightly flattened at the Poles*
2		What does the proverb you can't get a quart into a pint pot mean?	*You can't do the impossible*
3		How deep is the deepest part of the ocean: 1 mile, 3 miles, or 7 miles?	*7 miles (11,000 m)*
4		Can the world's largest bird fly?	*No. The ostrich is too big to fly*
5		Who was the British prime minister during World War II?	*Winston Churchill*
6		What do we mean when we say that someone has a sweet tooth?	*The person likes eating sweet things*
7		Do lines of latitude go from north to south or from east to west?	*East to west, parallel to the Equator*
8		Is there more of an iceberg under or over the water?	*Under*
9		Which is the largest bone in the human body – the shin bone, the thigh bone, or the hip bone?	*The thigh bone or femur*
10		Which animal builds a dam?	*The beaver*
11		What divides the Northern hemisphere from the Southern hemisphere?	*The Equator*
12		What causes the tides?	*The pull of the Moon and of the Sun*
13		What is the name of the war that took place between 1914 and 1918?	*World War I or the First World War*
14		What does an anaesthetic do?	*It stops you feeling pain*
15		Which is the world's smallest country?	*The Vatican in Rome*

Quiz 39
Question 12

Quiz 39
Question 4

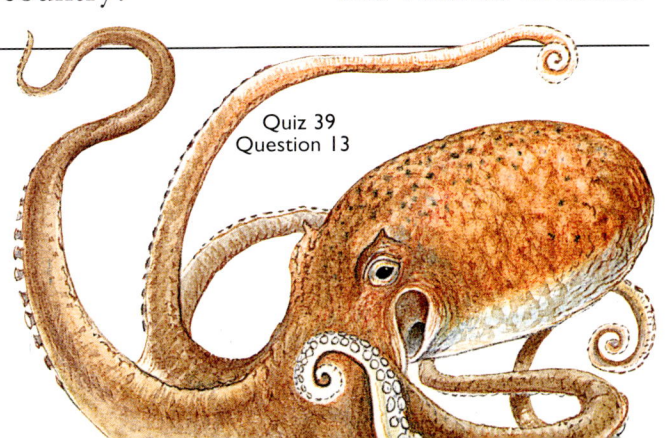

Quiz 39
Question 13

Quiz 41 Level 2

Questions

Answers

		Questions	Answers
1		Which sport is the most popular worldwide?	*Football (soccer)*
2		What is the capital of Belgium?	*Brussels*
3		What is minting?	*The craft of making coins*
4		What is the name of the most famous tower in Paris?	*The Eiffel Tower*
5		Why do hot air balloons float in the air?	*Because hot air is lighter than cold air*
6		Who lives in the White House?	*The president of the United States*
7		Which two countries is Mont Blanc on the border of?	*France and Italy*
8		What is veal?	*Calf meat*
9		Of what were the houses of the Three Little Pigs made?	*Straw, sticks and bricks*
10		What is the name of the musical instrument made of rows of bars that are struck with a hammer?	*A xylophone*
11		Which town did the Pied Piper rid of rats?	*Hamelin*
12		How does a marsupial carry its young?	*In its pouch*
13		How were Viking longboats powered?	*By a sail and oars*
14		What is a young swan called?	*A cygnet*
15		What is the name of the famous British queen who fought against the Romans?	*Boudicca*

Quiz 42
Question 3

Quiz 42
Question 1

Quiz 42 Level 2

Questions

Answers

	Questions	Answers
1	Give another name for a hog?	*A pig*
2	What do we call the disorder many people feel when they travel by boat?	*Sea sickness*
3	On which tree do acorns grow?	*The oak*
4	Which is the world's longest river – the Amazon, the Nile, or the Mississippi?	*The Nile*
5	Which day occurs only once every 4 years?	*February 29 (in a leap year)*
6	How many planets in our solar system support living things?	*Only the Earth*
7	Where are the Tropics?	*On or near the Equator*
8	What is a volunteer?	*Someone who offers to do something*
9	Are people animals?	*Yes, they are animals with complex brains*
10	What are twins?	*Two babies born at one birth*
11	What do we mean when we say that someone is *in hot water*?	*The person is in trouble*
12	Do we have a drum in our ear?	*Yes – the eardrum*
13	Where did the Vikings come from?	*From Scandinavia*
14	What is a lathe?	*A machine to shape wood or metal*
15	What did Johannes Gutenberg invent?	*Printing with movable type*

Quiz 41
Question 1

Quiz 41
Question 15

Quiz 43 Level 2

Questions

Answers

		Questions	Answers
1		What is paper made from?	Wood or cloth that is pulped and pressed
2		What does the proverb *don't count your chickens before they're hatched* mean?	Don't assume things until you're sure
3		Which pop group has sold more records and tapes than any other?	The Beatles
4		How many bones do adults have: 56, 106, 206?	206 bones
5		Where is Kennedy airport?	New York
6		Can a doctor cure a cold?	No. No cure for the cold has been found
7		Which ancient civilization invented paper, gunpowder, and silk-making?	The ancient Chinese
8		What is the capital of Scotland?	Edinburgh
9		What do we mean when we say that someone is *under the weather*?	The person is unwell
10		Which country's flag is called the Star Spangled Banner?	The United States of America
11		Who were the first people to live in New Zealand?	The Maoris
12		Where do we have lenses in our head?	In our eyes
13		Which is the fastest land animal – the hare, the gazelle, or the cheetah?	The cheetah
14		What did suffragettes fight for?	Votes for women
15		Who was Tutankhamun?	An Egyptian pharaoh

Quiz 44
Question 1

Quiz 44
Question 5

Quiz 44 Level 2

Questions

Answers

#		Question	Answer
1		What does a doctor use a stethoscope for?	*To listen to your breathing and heart*
2		What does it mean to *have forty winks*?	*It means to have a nap*
3		How many muscles do we have in our bodies – 69, 239, or 639?	*639 muscles*
4		Which was the first supersonic airliner?	*Concorde*
5		What is a Great Dane?	*A large dog*
6		What is albumen?	*The white of an egg*
7		Do the continents move?	*Yes, but very slowly*
8		What is braille?	*A system of dots read by the blind*
9		What does *take the bull by the horns* mean?	*Tackle a problem without fear*
10		How many sides does a triangle have?	*3*
11		When were the Middle Ages?	*From about the years 500 to 1460*
12		Which animal has the longest nose?	*The elephant (its trunk)*
13		What is the capital of Spain?	*Madrid*
14		What does sugar come from?	*Sugar cane and sugar beet*
15		What do Americans celebrate on July 4th?	*Independence day*

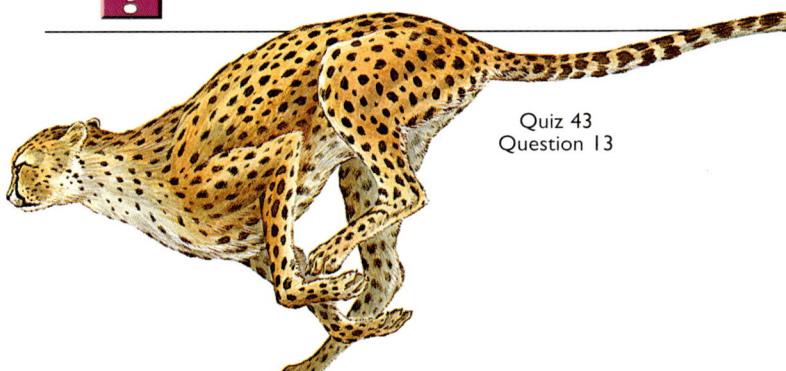

Quiz 43
Question 13

Quiz 43
Question 3

Quiz 45 Level 2

Questions

Answers

1	Which food substance most damages your teeth?	*Sugar*
2	In which city could you ride in a gondola?	*Venice in Italy*
3	What is formed when two lines meet?	*An angle*
4	Which are warmer – black clothes or white clothes?	*Black clothes because black absorbs heat*
5	Which mountain range contains the 13 highest mountains?	*The Himalayas*
6	What is at the centre of our solar system?	*The Sun*
7	Which American city suffered a huge earthquake in 1906?	*San Francisco*
8	What is the capital of Australia?	*Canberra*
9	Where is a rattlesnake's rattle?	*At the end of its tail*
10	What did George's marvellous medicine do?	*It made Grandma very tall*
11	Which animal is sometimes called a river horse?	*The hippopotamus*
12	Which game has smashes, rallies and lobs?	*Tennis*
13	Who was the president of the United States during World War II?	*Franklin D. Roosevelt*
14	What is deer meat called?	*Venison*
15	Who built an ark to survive a great flood?	*Noah*

Quiz 46
Question 4

Quiz 46
Question 1

Quiz 46 Level 2

	Questions	Answers
1	Where does a guinea pig store its food?	*In its cheeks*
2	What does a carnivore eat?	*Meat*
3	How many senses have we got?	*Five: sight, hearing, smell, taste, touch*
4	Which mythical creature is supposed to be half woman and half fish?	*A mermaid*
5	Which tree produces conkers?	*The horse chestnut*
6	What is another name for a shooting star?	*A meteor*
7	Where is the spinal cord?	*In your backbone*
8	Whose court was at Camelot?	*King Arthur's*
9	What are pedal pushers?	*A type of trouser*
10	Which line on the map divides east from west?	*The Greenwich meridian*
11	What kind of animals are the most intelligent?	*People*
12	What is a chronometer used for?	*Navigation*
13	What kind of land covers most of Australia?	*Desert*
14	What does *blow your top* mean?	*To be very angry*
15	Where is Hong Kong?	*Off the coast of China*

Quiz 45
Question 11

Quiz 47 Level 2

Questions

Answers

#	Question	Answer
1	Which elephants have larger ears: African or Indian?	*African*
2	What do viruses cause?	*Diseases such as colds and measles*
3	What is *ju-jitsu*?	*A form of wrestling developed in Japan*
4	Could you jump higher on the Moon or on Earth?	*On the Moon*
5	What do people receive Oscars for?	*Achievements in films*
6	Why do spiders build webs?	*To catch their prey*
7	Which countries make up Scandinavia?	*Norway, Sweden and Denmark*
8	When do eclipses of the Sun occur?	*If the Moon hides the Sun from the Earth*
9	What does *to throw in the towel* mean?	*To admit defeat*
10	Who led the Roundheads in the English Civil War?	*Oliver Cromwell*
11	Who wrote *The Twits*?	*Roald Dahl*
12	In which sport can you make a hole-in-one?	*Golf*
13	What was the code name for the day the Allied forces landed in Normandy during World War II?	*D-Day*
14	Which dinosaur had spiky plates along its back and ate plants?	*Stegosaurus*
15	What is the collective name for knives, forks and spoons?	*Cutlery*

Quiz 48
Question 3

Quiz 48
Question 14

Quiz 48 Level 2

	Questions	Answers
1	What is the difference between amateurs and professionals in sport?	Amateurs aren't paid professionals are
2	What is the difference between *hail* and *hale*?	'Hail' is frozen rain; 'hale' means healthy
3	What was a blunderbuss?	A kind of gun
4	*Ding dong bell* – where's pussy?	In the well
5	What is the name for a tube which carries blood to the heart?	A vein
6	Why do we have seasons every year?	Because the Earth is tilted on its axis
7	What is cheese made from?	Milk
8	What happens if a football player gets a red card?	The player is sent off
9	What does a bud grow into?	A flower or a leaf
10	Which country produces Camembert cheese?	France
11	Who is remembered for the Gunpowder Plot?	Guy Fawkes
12	Do female reindeer have antlers?	Yes
13	Which countries make up Great Britain?	England, Scotland and Wales
14	Which melon has pink flesh and black seeds?	A water melon
15	What is 25 percent of 16?	4

Quiz 47
Question 8

Quiz 47
Question 6

Quiz 49 Level 2

	Questions	Answers
1	Why do some desert plants have very long roots?	*To reach water deep underground*
2	Which airport handles more international aircraft than any other airport in the world?	*London Heathrow*
3	Which is the only mammal that flies?	*The bat*
4	What does CD stand for?	*Compact Disk*
5	Which famous painting by Leonardo da Vinci is known for its smile?	*The Mona Lisa*
6	What is biology the science of?	*Life*
7	What is produced in a blast furnace?	*Iron*
8	What is the target ball in a game of bowls called?	*The jack*
9	Why do astronauts on the Moon need to take oxygen with them?	*Because there is no air on the Moon*
10	Which is the highest mountain in Britain?	*Ben Nevis in Scotland*
11	Shakespeare wrote a play about which Roman general?	*Julius Caesar*
12	The Carribean Sea is part of which ocean?	*The Atlantic*
13	Who said: *Never in the field of human conflict was so much owed by so many to so few*?	*Winston Churchill*
14	How would you measure a perimeter?	*By adding the lengths of the sides*
15	In which war did the Roundheads fight the Cavaliers?	*The English Civil War*

Quiz 50
Question 6

Quiz 50
Question 13

Quiz 50 Level 2

Questions

Answers

		Questions	Answers
1		What is a hangar?	*A building for keeping aircraft*
2		What is 50 percent of 50?	*25*
3		John Lennon, Ringo Starr and George Harrison were three of the Beatles. Who was the fourth?	*Paul McCartney*
4		What is the study of plants called?	*Botany*
5		Who founded the Boy Scouts movement?	*Robert Baden-Powell*
6		Which are you most likely to see at night: a butterfly or a moth?	*A moth*
7		In which sea is the island of Crete?	*The Mediterranean*
8		Who wrote Robinson Crusoe?	*Daniel Defoe*
9		What is chlorophyll?	*Green substance found in plants*
10		What does a disinfectant do?	*Kills germs*
11		Which city were the Crusaders fighting for control of?	*Jerusalem*
12		What is the name for a small explosive charge that sets off a bomb?	*A detonator*
13		Who was the only ruler of Britain who ruled instead of a king or a queen?	*Oliver Cromwell*
14		Which is the world's largest country?	*The Russian Federation*
15		Which spiny plants grow in deserts?	*Cacti (singular, cactus)*

Quiz 49
Question 3

Quiz 49
Question 11

Quiz 49
Question 4

Quiz 51 Level 2

	Questions	Answers
1	What are young goats called?	*Kids*
2	How many holes are there on a golf course?	*18*
3	Currants, raisins and sultanas are all dried what?	*Grapes*
4	What is the force that pulls everything towards the Earth?	*Gravity*
5	Which German brothers wrote a famous collection of fairy tales?	*The brothers Grimm*
6	How many humps does a Bactrian camel have?	*2*
7	What is the capital of Denmark?	*Copenhagen*
8	What happens at the Edinburgh Festival?	*Arts events such as drama, music, dance*
9	Which English monarch led the defeat of the Spanish Armada?	*Queen Elizabeth I*
10	Which is the longest river entirely in England?	*The Severn*
11	What is a private eye?	*A private detective*
12	Who pioneered the Theory of Evolution?	*Charles Darwin*
13	Early pens were made from birds' feathers. What were they called?	*Quill pens*
14	If someone has a *nest egg*, what do they have?	*Savings put aside*
15	In which year did England and Wales unite with Scotland; 1607, 1707 or 1807?	*1707*

Quiz 52
Question 4

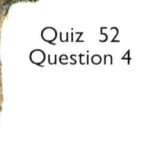
Quiz 52
Question 8

Quiz 52 Level 2

Questions | ## Answers

#	Question	Answer
1	Where is the biggest and busiest McDonald's – New York, Paris, Moscow or London?	*In Moscow!*
2	What are the White Cliffs of Dover made from?	*Chalk*
3	What do you call a curved stick used by the Aborigines in Australia for hunting?	*A boomerang*
4	Which kind of cat is fawn-coloured and has blue eyes?	*A Siamese cat*
5	What is the capital of Egypt?	*Cairo*
6	Are dolphins a kind of whale?	*Yes*
7	Pines, cedars and yews are all what kind of tree?	*Conifers*
8	Who wrote *David Copperfield*?	*Charles Dickens*
9	Which precious stone is green?	*Emerald*
10	Who is Mickey Mouse's girlfriend?	*Minnie Mouse*
11	Which river flows through Paris?	*The Seine*
12	Who led Britain for much of World War I?	*Lloyd George*
13	Do like magnetic poles attract each other or push each other apart?	*They push each other apart*
14	Which battle did William the Conqueror win in 1066?	*The battle of Hastings*
15	What do you call a toy with mirrors that creates random regular patterns?	*A kaleidoscope*

Quiz 51
Question 6

Quiz 51
Question 9

Quiz 53 Level 2

Questions

Answers

		Question	Answer
1		Which insect transmits malaria?	The mosquito
2		What does *smell a rat* mean?	To suspect that something is wrong
3		How long is a leap year?	366 days
4		If a person is short-sighted, do they have trouble seeing nearby objects or objects at a distance?	Objects at a distance
5		What is the capital of Japan?	Tokyo
6		Which parts of a tree trap sunlight and make food for the tree?	The leaves
7		What is a loom used for?	Weaving cloth
8		Which American president vowed to put men on the Moon before 1970?	John F. Kennedy
9		What is the word *fax* short for?	Facsimile
10		What is the main religion of India?	Hinduism
11		How did Adolf Hitler die?	He committed suicide
12		Where is Cape Horn?	At the southern tip of South America
13		What is economic inflation?	A period of rising prices
14		What vegetable keeps away vampires?	Garlic
15		Which English king established the Church of England?	Henry VIII

Quiz 54
Question 4

Quiz 54
Question 12

Quiz 54 Level 2

Questions

Answers

#	Question	Answer
1	Which rodent is covered with long, sharp, black and white spikes called quills?	*The porcupine*
2	What kind of boats have rigging?	*Sailing boats*
3	Does a whale breathe air?	*Yes*
4	What is another name for pingpong?	*Table tennis*
5	What do Milton, Wordsworth and Roger McGough have in common?	*They are all poets*
6	What is the device for showing the movement of stars and planets on a curved ceiling?	*A planetarium*
7	What were Henry Morgan and Captain Kidd?	*Pirates*
8	When did King Wenceslas last look out?	*On the feast of St Stephen*
9	Who invented radio?	*Guglielmo Marconi*
10	Which queen was called Bloody Mary?	*Queen Mary I*
11	Which strait connects the Mediterranean to the Atlantic Ocean?	*The Strait of Gibraltar*
12	Which prehistoric reptiles died out 65 million years ago?	*Dinosaurs*
13	Why is a mocking bird so called?	*Because it mimics other creatures' cries*
14	Who founded the Muslim religion?	*Muhammad*
15	Which is the highest mountain in Europe?	*Mt Elbrus (in the Russian Federation)*

Quiz 53
Question 1

Quiz 53
Question 15

Quiz 53
Question 14

Quiz 55 Level 2

Questions

Answers

		Question	Answer
1		Which missionary organization is structured like an army with ranks and uniforms?	*The Salvation Army*
2		It is the smallest fish of the herring family and we usually buy it in tins. What is it?	*The sardine*
3		What is the headquarters of London`s Metropolitan Police called?	*Scotland Yard*
4		Which small fish hangs upright in the water, holding on to seaweed stems with its tail?	*The sea horse*
5		Which plant is the emblem of Ireland?	*The shamrock*
6		Which language is spoken in Rome?	*Italian*
7		A cricket ball and a tennis ball are dropped from the top of a building: which hits the ground first?	*They hit the ground at the same time*
8		In which continent is the Zambezi River?	*Africa*
9		The average roomful of air weighs 15, 25, 35, or 45 kg?	*45 kg*
10		Which is the largest of the apes?	*The gorilla*
11		How many degrees are there in a right angle?	*90 degrees*
12		In which building in central Rome did the Romans hold contests between gladiators	*The Colosseum*
13		What is the capital of Canada?	*Ottawa*
14		Who was Prince Albert married to?	*Queen Victoria*
15		What was dropped on Hiroshima?	*The first atom bomb*

Quiz 56
Question 12

Quiz 56
Question 4

Quiz 56 Level 2

Questions

Answers

		Questions	Answers
1		Which group of sea mammals have flippers for swimming, live in herds and *bark*?	*Seals*
2		What do we mean when we say *curiosity killed the cat*?	*Being curious can lead you into trouble*
3		Who was Moses' brother?	*Aaron*
4		Which Scottish doctor explored Africa in the nineteenth century?	*David Livingstone*
5		Which tall plant has huge, yellow flowers and has seeds that are rich in oil?	*The sunflower*
6		The litre is the metric measure of what?	*Capacity*
7		Who were Pavlova, Nijinsky, and Fonteyn?	*Famous ballet stars*
8		As time goes on the human brain is getting bigger. True or false?	*True*
9		Which country produces the most coffee?	*Brazil*
10		The beam, the arch, and the suspension are three kinds of what?	*Bridges*
11		Which river do the Great Lakes flow into?	*The St Lawrence River*
12		What type of insect is a Red Admiral?	*A butterfly*
13		Where is Jesus said to have been born?	*Bethlehem*
14		What did Hitler, Mussolini, and Stalin have in common?	*They were all dictators*
15		Which mammals use echoes to fly in the dark?	*Bats*

Quiz 55
Question 10

Quiz 55
Question 8

Quiz 57 Level 2

Questions

Answers

		Questions	Answers
1		The dove returned to Noah with what?	An olive branch
2		Who were the first people to grow potatoes, maize, tomatoes, and tobacco?	The Native Americans
3		What were V1s?	German guided missiles
4		Which country is New Mexico in?	The USA
5		Who wrote *Pride and Prejudice*?	Jane Austen
6		Where is Fiji?	In the Pacific Ocean
7		If someone's bank account is in the red what does it mean?	The person owes the bank
8		If the length of a cube's side is 2 cm, what is its volume?	8 cubic cm
9		Which fish can fly?	Flying fish
10		What are cirrus, cumulus and cirrostratus examples of?	Clouds
11		Which country did Britain fight in 1982 for the Falkland Islands?	Argentina
12		What does a bird have that no other animal has?	Feathers
13		Which cereal crop grows under water?	Rice
14		Where did Horatio Nelson die?	Trafalgar
15		What do we mean when we say that people are *as thick as thieves*?	They are very friendly

Quiz 58
Question 4

Quiz 58
Question 13

Quiz 58 Level 2

	Questions	Answers
1	What is the name for twins joined together at some part of their bodies?	*Siamese twins*
2	What does your bladder do?	*Collects and stores urine*
3	Does a flea have wings?	*No*
4	Which country does the island of Corsica belong to?	*France*
5	How did Mahatma Gandhi die?	*He was shot by a fellow Hindu*
6	What are rings, parallel bars and the pommel horse?	*Gymnastic exercises for men*
7	What do you call small flakes of dead skin in the hair caused by a disorder of the scalp glands?	*Dandruff*
8	Who was Robinson Crusoe's companion?	*Man Friday*
9	What is the *Tour de France*?	*A cycle race*
10	Which country was at war with Iran for 8 years from 1980?	*Iraq*
11	What is the currency of Japan?	*The yen*
12	In which disease do some of the body's cells go out of control and multiply?	*Cancer*
13	What are hock, withers, muzzle, and pattern?	*They are all parts of a horse*
14	What are Orion, Leo, Lyra, and Gemini?	*They are constellations of stars*
15	How many people dance a *pas de deux*?	*2*

Quiz 57
Question 9

Quiz 57
Question 3

Quiz 59 Level 2

Questions

Answers

		Question	Answer
1		Algebra, calculus and geometry are three branches of which subject?	*Mathematics*
2		Which city do Muslims face when they pray?	*Mecca in Saudi Arabia*
3		How does a dog cool itself down?	*By panting*
4		What two colours do you mix to make green?	*Blue and yellow*
5		Which are the three most important fuels?	*Coal, oil, and natural gas*
6		What does a flag raised at half-mast mean?	*People are mourning someone's death*
7		What do ants, bees and termites have in common?	*They live in highly organized groups*
8		What is the difference between maps and charts?	*Maps show the land, charts cover the sea*
9		What is theology?	*The study of religion*
10		Where are British monarchs crowned?	*Westminster Abbey*
11		What was the mass killings of Jews in Nazi Germany called?	*The Holocaust*
12		What is copper mostly used for?	*To make electrical wires*
13		Which brass instrument has a slide section?	*The trombone*
14		To whom was Anne Hathaway married?	*William Shakespeare*
15		What are the horns of a stag called?	*Antlers*

Quiz 60
Question 7

Quiz 60
Question 9

Quiz 60 Level 2

Questions

Answers

		Questions	Answers
1		How many sides are there on the base of a pyramid?	Four sides, making a square
2		What is the name for the Hindu festival of lights?	Divali
3		What is the world's population? More than 3 billion, 4 billion, 5 billion, or 6 billion?	More than 6 billion
4		What is three-quarters of 16?	12
5		What is the name for the masses of tiny plants and animals that drift in the sea?	Plankton
6		Manhattan Island is at the centre of which city?	New York
7		What is the Earth's closest neighbour in space?	The Moon
8		Which Roman god of war had a month named after him?	Mars – March
9		Who was the *Führer*?	Adolf Hitler
10		What is the long digestive tube which begins at the stomach and ends at the anus called?	The intestine
11		*Red sky at night* is whose delight?	Shepherds'
12		Which current UK coin has a diameter of 3 cm?	The 50-pence piece
13		What is called the ship of the desert?	The camel
14		What was Aesop famous for writing?	Fables
15		Which country was Lenin leader of?	The USSR

Quiz 59
Question 13

Quiz 59
Question 14

Quiz 61 Level 2

Questions

Answers

		Question	Answer
1		How many strings does a violin have?	4
2		Where do people pay in *deutschmarks*?	*In Germany*
3		Which are your incisors?	*The flat front teeth*
4		How many sides has a twenty-pence piece?	7
5		Do butterflies or moths rest with their wings spread out flat?	*Moths. Butterflies hold theirs upright*
6		Which Hollywood actor became president of the United States?	*Ronald Reagan*
7		A rowing eight has a ninth member. What is he or she called?	*The cox or coxwain*
8		Is a baboon an ape or a monkey?	*A monkey*
9		What did Prohibition ban in America?	*The sale of alcohol*
10		Which is the smallest stringed instrument in the modern orchestra?	*The violin*
11		In which ocean is the island of St Helena?	*The Atlantic*
12		Which country did Hitler invade in 1939?	*Poland*
13		What are the words of a song called?	*The lyrics*
14		What is the commonest produce of insects that we eat?	*Honey*
15		What is an Islamic place of worship called?	*A mosque*

Quiz 62
Question 10

Quiz 62 Level 2

Questions		Answers
1	What are the vault, beam, floor and asymmetric bars?	*Gymnastic exercises for women*
2	Which creatures have a head, a thorax, and an abdomen?	*Insects*
3	What are the three states of matter?	*Solids, liquids, and gases*
4	What are *Pravda, Le Monde,* and the *Washington Post*?	*Newspapers*
5	What are barnacles?	*A kind of shellfish*
6	What is 0.75 of 24?	*18*
7	Who is Jayne Torvill's partner?	*Christopher Dean*
8	Who was the first Danish king of England?	*Canute*
9	What is another name for gypsies?	*Romanies or travellers*
10	What kind of plane was a Lancaster?	*A bomber*
11	When is the best time to see badgers?	*After sunset*
12	How do Americans spell *grey*?	*Gray*
13	Where do people pay with *pesetas*?	*Spain*
14	Who created Jeremy Fisher and Peter Rabbit?	*Beatrix Potter*
15	Where would you find a retina, cornea, and iris?	*In the eye*

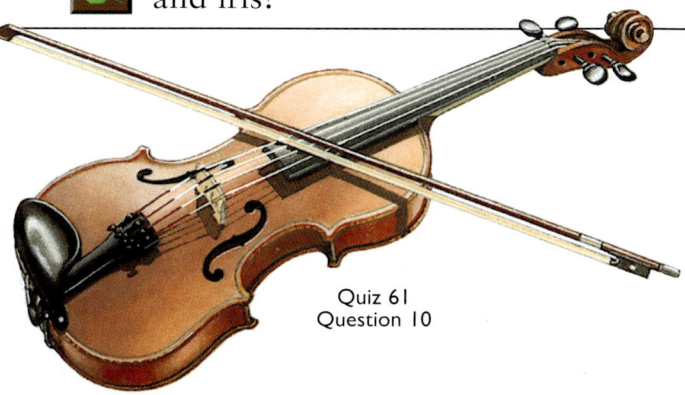

Quiz 61
Question 10

Quiz 61
Question 6

Quiz 63 Level 2

	Questions	Answers
1	What is a gaucho?	*A South American cowboy*
2	In which sport is the Davis Cup awarded?	*Tennis*
3	Which statue is at the centre of Piccadilly Circus in London?	*Eros*
4	Who ate Turkey Lurkey?	*Foxy Loxy*
5	Which food is eaten by most of the world's people?	*Rice*
6	Pneumonia affects which part of the body?	*The lungs*
7	What is the opposite of honest?	*Dishonest*
8	Where in your body would you find your adenoids?	*At the back of the nose and throat*
9	What is 0.2 x 10?	*2*
10	Who was Al Capone?	*An American gangster*
11	The Secretary-General is the head of which organization?	*The United Nations*
12	Which German city was divided by a wall?	*Berlin*
13	Who went to sea in *a beautiful pea-green boat*?	*The owl and the pussy-cat*
14	In which country is the ski resort of St Moritz?	*Switzerland*
15	Which is Islam's most holy city?	*Mecca*

Quiz 64
Question 9

Quiz 64
Question 3

Quiz 64 Level 2

Questions

Answers

1		Which country is known for its mountains, watches and chocolate?	*Switzerland*
2		How is plywood made?	*By gluing thin layers of wood together*
3		In which sport was Rocky Marciano unbeatable?	*Boxing*
4		Which of these is not an African country: Gambia, Ghana, Guyana, Congo?	*Guyana*
5		Which metal costs three times as much as gold?	*Platinum*
6		How does the possum try to avoid capture?	*By pretending to be dead*
7		How many spots are on a six-sided dice?	*21*
8		Which is the highest numbered segment on a dart board?	*20*
9		Which is the only bird that can fly backwards and hover?	*The humming bird*
10		In which country is the Algarve?	*Portugal*
11		There are no such things as Vampire bats. True or false?	*False*
12		What do Americans call a sweet shop?	*A candy store*
13		If I have 14 sweets and give 3 to one friend and 2 to another. How many do I have left?	*9*
14		How many years are there between 15 BC and AD 15 ?	*30*
15		Julius Caesar sailed from Gaul to England. What is Gaul now called?	*France*

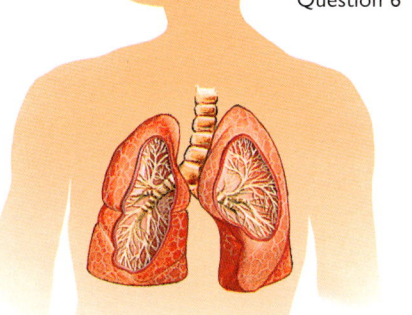

Quiz 63
Question 6

Quiz 63
Question 1

Quiz 65 Level 2

	Questions	Answers
1	Which musical instrument consists of a long pipe and is played by Aborigines?	*The didgeridoo*
2	What do you dry to get a prune?	*A plum*
3	Who were the greatest road-builders of the ancient world?	*The Romans*
4	Which substance makes fireworks explode?	*Gunpowder*
5	Which black and white seabird has a red, blue, and yellow bill?	*The puffin*
6	What are your sinuses? Quiz 66 Question 3	*Four cavities in the bones of your skull*
7	Which famous New York skyscraper was for some time the world's highest building?	*The Empire State Building*
8	When used for lighting, what colour does neon gas give out?	*A brilliant orange-red*
9	Six nations produce two-thirds of the world's oranges. Name three of them.	*US, Brazil, Mexico, Spain, Italy, Israel*
10	What does it mean to *take the plunge*?	*Decide to do something risky*
11	In which American state is Disneyland?	*California*
12	What does it mean to *nip something in the bud*?	*Stop something before it begins*
13	Which big bird has long legs, a graceful neck, and pink plumage?	*The flamingo*
14	Which religion did the Romans adopt in the AD 300s?	*Christianity*
15	Is an egress a kind of bird?	*No – it's an exit!*

Quiz 66 Question 9

Quiz 66 Level 2

Questions

Answers

1	Which group of animals has hair and feeds its young on the mother's milk?	The mammals
2	What is our galaxy called?	The Milky Way
3	What is the mongoose famed for killing?	Snakes
4	Who was Henry Moore?	A great British sculptor
5	What do three dots represent in the Morse Code?	The letter S
6	What is noise measured in?	Decibels
7	Who was Juliet's lover in Shakespeare's play?	Romeo
8	Tibet is ruled by which country?	China
9	Which brightly-coloured tropical bird has an enormous orange beak?	The toucan
10	What is the capital of Turkey?	Istanbul
11	Where is urine made in your body?	In your kidneys
12	Which naval hero won the battles of Cape St Vincent, the Nile, and Copenhagen?	Horatio Nelson
13	Which ocean lies between Africa, Asia, Australia, and Antarctica?	The Indian Ocean
14	What is the masculine of goose?	Gander
15	Which ancient people invented paper?	The Chinese

Quiz 65
Question 5

Quiz 65
Question 2

Quiz 67 Level 2

Questions

Answers

#	Question	Answer
1	In the US, pumpkin pie is a traditional dish on which day?	*Thanksgiving Day*
2	In which city is the Louvre?	*Paris*
3	On which day of the week does Pancake Day fall?	*Tuesday*
4	Which rodent spread the Plague?	*The rat*
5	Alligators, crocodiles, and snakes are all what?	*Reptiles*
6	Which rock is formed from grains of sand?	*Sandstone*
7	Which is the most common animal in Australia?	*The sheep*
8	Sinking the black ball in snooker scores how many points?	*7*
9	What does *supersonic* mean?	*Faster than the speed of sound*
10	What are your biceps?	*Muscles in your arms*
11	What are you doing if you are doing the quick-step?	*Dancing*
12	How many sides has a cube?	*6*
13	What does *you scratch my back and I'll scratch yours* mean?	*Help me out and I'll help you*
14	Which of the Seven Wonders of the World still stands?	*The Great Pyramid, Egypt*
15	Which Houses fought the Wars of the Roses?	*York and Lancaster*

Quiz 68
Question 10

Quiz 68
Question 5

Quiz 68 Level 2

Questions

Answers

		Questions	Answers
1		What is a census?	*An official count of the population*
2		What is special about a catamaran?	*It is a boat with two hulls*
3		Which edible blue-black mollusc is found in clusters on coastal rocks?	*The mussel*
4		What is the capital of Israel?	*Jerusalem*
5		Which animal is yellow with black spots and is called a panther in India?	*A leopard*
6		What colour is jade?	*Usually green*
7		What do we call the technique of creating a sleep-like trance in people?	*Hypnosis*
8		What is a dromedary?	*A one-humped camel bred for riding*
9		What does *make a clean breast of it* mean?	*Confess everything*
10		Who built the famous Model T car?	*Henry Ford*
11		What were seagoing galleys?	*Roman long boats powered by rowers*
12		What is the French city of Chartres famous for?	*Its cathedral*
13		Stockholm is the capital of which country?	*Sweden*
14		What do you call someone who comes from Sweden?	*A Swede*
15		What is *horse sense*?	*Common sense*

Quiz 67
Question 7

Quiz 67
Question 12

Quiz 69 Level 2

Questions

Answers

		Question	Answer
1		Where is the Grand National run?	*Aintree, near Liverpool*
2		Why are ladybirds useful to gardeners?	*They eat insects, especially greenfly*
3		Where might you find the Abominable snowman?	*In the Himalaya Mountains*
4		What are secateurs?	*Pruning shears*
5		Which mountains divide Spain from France?	*The Pyrenees*
6		Howard Carter discovered which Egyptian pharaoh's tomb in 1922?	*Tutankhamun*
7		How many players are there in an ice hockey team?	*Six and the goalkeeper*
8		What is a French castle or large mansion called?	*A château*
9		What is a bream?	*A fish*
10		Which instrument did Chopin play?	*The piano*
11		What is the crown of a tooth?	*The part above the gum*
12		*Elementary, my dear Watson?* Who said that?	*Sherlock Holmes*
13		Which colours make up the Irish flag?	*Orange, green and white*
14		Which dictator ruled Iraq during the 1980s and 1990s?	*Saddam Hussein*
15		Which speckled freshwater fish belongs to the salmon family?	*The trout*

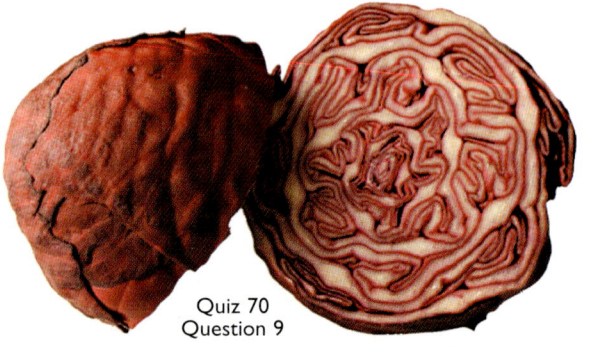

Quiz 70
Question 9

Quiz 70
Question 10

Quiz 70 Level 2

Questions

Answers

		Questions	Answers
1		Which is the largest seaport in northwest England?	*Liverpool*
2		Who led the Israelites out of captivity in Egypt?	*Moses*
3		What is the correct term for ancient Egyptian picture-writing?	*Hieroglyphic script*
4		Which process for preserving food was named after Louis Pasteur?	*Pasteurization*
5		Which fungus is used to make bread, beer, and wine?	*Yeast*
6		How many people are in a quintet?	*5*
7		Who was Saladin?	*Muslim leader who fought the Crusaders*
8		Which Indian and African dog-like animal makes an uncanny laughing noise?	*The hyena*
9		What is the main ingredient in *sauerkraut*?	*Cabbage*
10		Which animals shed their antlers and grow new ones every year?	*Deer*
11		What proportion of the air is oxygen – one fifth, one eighth, or one tenth?	*One fifth*
12		What is to *practise what you preach*?	*To behave as you tell others to behave*
13		Which age came after the Stone Age?	*Bronze Age*
14		What, according to the nursery rhyme, are little girls made of?	*Sugar and spice and all things nice*
15		What is 20 percent of 100?	*20*

Quiz 69
Question 9

Quiz 69
Question 6

Quiz 71 Level 2

Questions

Answers

1	Why is pain useful?	*To warn us when something is wrong*
2	Dates, coconuts, and raffia all come from what?	*Palm trees*
3	What does the Jewish Passover commemorate?	*The escape from Egypt under Moses*
4	Which large bear-like animal has black and white fur and eats bamboo shoots?	*The Giant panda*
5	Who wrote the operas *Don Giovanni* and the *Magic Flute*?	*Mozart*
6	Where is the volcano Mount Etna?	*Italy (on the island of Sicily)*
7	Which game has knights, castles, and bishops?	*Chess*
8	Which sea creature squirts out an inky fluid to escape from an enemy?	*The octopus*
9	What have taken the place of glass valves in radios?	*Transistors*
10	Which large sea-mammal has two long tusks?	The walrus
11	Which cereal grain is grown in paddy fields?	Rice
12	What does *ask no questions and you'll hear no lies* mean?	*Don't show curiosity*
13	How often in 24 hours does the tide rise and fall?	*Twice*
14	What does *ecstatic* mean?	*Happy*
15	When did World War I begin?	*1914*

Quiz 72
Question 10

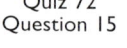

Quiz 72
Question 15

Quiz 72 Level 2

Questions

Answers

#	Question	Answer
1	What are a clove hitch and a reef?	*Types of knot*
2	The world's fourth largest island lies off the east coast of Africa. What is it called?	*Madagascar*
3	What made the craters on the Moon?	*Meteorites*
4	What kind of music did Louis Armstrong and Duke Ellington play?	*Jazz*
5	Which boy didn't want to grow up?	*Peter Pan*
6	Who were the Boers?	*Dutch settlers in South Africa*
7	Which is Britain's only poisonous snake?	*The adder*
8	Why does water flow downhill?	*Because it is pulled by gravity*
9	Is the Sun an unusual kind of star?	*No, it is quite ordinary*
10	What are the citrus fruits?	*Oranges, lemons, grapefruits, limes*
11	Which country was led by General de Gaulle?	*France*
12	Why are flowers coloured?	*To attract insects which transfer pollen*
13	What do Americans call a car-park?	*A parking lot*
14	What was remarkable about Matilda?	*She had magical powers*
15	What is a male chicken called?	*A cockerel*

Quiz 71
Question 4

Quiz 71
Question 7

Quiz 73 Level 2

Questions

Answers

1		Woodwind, percussion and brass are three sections of an orchestra. What is the fourth?	*Strings*
2		What do we call a tropical fruit with yellow skin, yellow flesh, and spiky leaves out of the top?	*The pineapple*
3		What does *eccentric* mean?	*Different from most others*
4		What happened to Anne Boleyn?	*She was beheaded*
5		Which one of these materials will a magnet pick up: paper, iron, aluminium, wood?	*Iron*
6		If you *go aft* in a boat, where do you go?	*To the stern – the back*
7		What is an extinct volcano?	*A volcano that no longer erupts*
8		A geriatric ward in a hospital takes care of what kind of people?	*Old people*
9		What breed are Eskimo dogs?	*Huskies*
10		What garment, worn mainly by Hindu women, is made by wrapping cloth?	*The sari*
11		Which part of the body is affected by conjunctivitis?	*The eye*
12		Which harbour did the Japanese attack on December 7, 1941?	*Pearl Harbor, Hawaii*
13		Which sport is Le Mans famous for?	*Motor racing*
14		Which king of England was called The Lionheart?	*Richard I*
15		What is the name of Moscow's chief square?	*Red Square*

Quiz 74
Question 1

Quiz 74
Question 15

Quiz 74 Level 2

	Questions	Answers
1	Which English king reigned from 1660 to 1685?	*Charles II*
2	What is the minimum school-leaving age in Britain?	*16*
3	Which dwarf could spin straw into gold?	*Rumpelstiltskin*
4	What is one third of 51?	*17*
5	Which is the lee side of a boat?	*The side away from the wind*
6	Which country's national symbol is a thistle?	*Scotland*
7	What is a Jewish place of worship called?	*A synagogue*
8	What crop does sweet corn come from?	*Maize*
9	Who saw Cock Robin die?	*The fly, with his little eye*
10	What colour are cornflowers?	*Blue*
11	Did the Crusades take place in the Middle Ages, the Dark Ages, or the Renaissance?	*The Middle Ages*
12	What is the climate like in a tropical forest – hot and dry or hot and wet?	*Hot and wet*
13	Which famous London museum is named after a queen of England and her husband?	*The Victoria and Albert Museum*
14	How many millilitres are in half a litre?	*500*
15	Which fish makes spectacular leaps to return to its birthplace?	*The salmon*

Quiz 73
Question 2

Quiz 73
Question 14

Quiz 75 Level 2

Questions

1. Who are the Harlem Globe Trotters?
2. What is 15 divided by 2.5?
3. What is the study of history through objects called?
4. What is the singular of dice?
5. Which title is given to the eldest son of an English sovereign?
6. What man-made objects orbit the Earth and help with communication?
7. Does a west wind blow from the west or to the west?
8. Who was the Roman god of the sea?
9. How many minutes are there between 10.15 and 11.05?
10. Which of these words is a noun: *hopped, laughing, road, because*?
11. Which is nearer to London – Glasgow or Paris?
12. What kind of creature can unhinge its jaws to swallow its prey?
13. Who was Benjamin Disraeli?
14. Which rogue had a hook instead of a hand?
15. How many legs has a quadruped?

Answers

1. An all-black basketball team
2. 6
3. Archaeology
4. Die
5. Prince of Wales
6. Satellites
7. It blows from the west
8. Neptune
9. 50 minutes
10. Road
11. Paris
12. The snake
13. A British prime minister
14. Captain Hook in Peter Pan
15. 4

Quiz 76
Question 8

Quiz 76
Question 15

Quiz 76 Level 2

Questions

Answers

#		Question	Answer
1		What is curious about a Manx cat's tail?	*It doesn't have one*
2		Who are the Wallabies?	*The Australian rugby union team*
3		Which country is the largest consumer of tea in the world?	*Ireland*
4		Is a bird an animal?	*Yes*
5		For what does GMT stand?	*Greenwich Mean Time*
6		What kind of person was Scrooge?	*Mean*
7		How many noughts has a million?	*6*
8		Which animal faded away, leaving only its grin?	*The Cheshire Cat*
9		What is the highest number on a playing card?	*10*
10		What might you find in an oyster?	*A pearl*
11		In what sport do you butterfly or crawl?	*Swimming*
12		Who was William Gladstone?	*A British prime minister*
13		What is a Camberwell Beauty?	*A butterfly*
14		In photography, what is a negative?	*Developed, unprinted film*
15		Which American civil rights leader was assassinated in 1968?	*Martin Luther King*

Quiz 75
Question 1

Quiz 75
Question 12

Quiz 77 Level 3

Questions

Answers

#	Question	Answer
1	What is the name for a straight line that joins one corner of a square to the opposite corner?	*A diagonal*
2	Looking towards a ship's bow, is the port side on left or the right?	*The left side*
3	People drink the fermented juice of apples. What is it called?	*Cider*
4	Who was Sherlock Holmes's assistant?	*Dr Watson*
5	Is the Sun mainly solid, like the Earth, or liquid or gas?	*Gas (mostly hydrogen)*
6	What is the name for a large, slow-moving mass of ice on the surface of the land?	*A glacier*
7	What is the national bird of New Zealand?	*The kiwi*
8	What word means a family or species of animals that has died out?	*Extinct*
9	Who was Good Queen Bess?	*Queen Elizabeth I of England*
10	Which tree is the most massive?	*A Californian Redwood*
11	Which reptiles ruled the world for over 160 million years?	*Dinosaurs*
12	What do you call people who study animals?	*Zoologists*
13	Who wrote the music for *The Lion King*?	*Elton John*
14	Which is the Red Planet?	*Mars*
15	Where is the Grand Canyon, the world's longest gorge?	*In Arizona, USA*

Quiz 78
Question 14

Quiz 78
Question 4

Quiz 78 Level 3

	Questions	Answers
1	What country's flag is a red circle on a white background?	*Japan*
2	What does RSVP mean on an invitation?	*Please reply*
3	What is the capital of India?	*New Delhi*
4	Which planet is named after the Roman god of water?	*Neptune*
5	How many corners does a cube have?	*8*
6	What is a vertebrate?	*An animal which has a backbone*
7	Where are the lands of the midnight sun?	*The Arctic and Antarctic*
8	Who is the patron saint of Wales?	*Saint David*
9	Who was the first man on the Moon?	*Neil Armstrong*
10	Who reached America in 1492?	*Christopher Columbus*
11	What does an entomologist study?	*Insects*
12	How many limbs has an octopus?	*8*
13	Which is the noun in this sentence: *The bird is black*?	*Bird*
14	What is another name for a cupola?	*A dome*
15	What is the square root of 64?	*8*

Quiz 77
Question 11

Quiz 77
Question 14

Quiz 79 Level 3

Questions

Answers

		Question	Answer
1		Which was the first artificial satellite?	*The Russian Sputnik*
2		What is the most common name in Britain?	*Smith*
3		What is the name of the ancient monument consisting of a ring of stones on Salisbury Plain?	*Stonehenge*
4		Do flightless birds have wings?	*Yes*
5		Which is colder, the North Pole or the South Pole?	*The South Pole*
6		What is the hardest natural substance?	*Diamond*
7		What is the name for a crack in the Earth's surface that spouts boiling water at intervals?	*A geyser*
8		Which short war was fought in Kuwait and Iraq in 1991?	*The Gulf War*
9		What is the name of the ancient Egyptian kings?	*Pharaohs*
10		Which continent has most people?	*Asia*
11		What does *love* mean in tennis?	*Nil*
12		What is a word for parsley, sage, mint and basil?	*Herbs*
13		Which precious stones are found in oysters?	*Pearls*
14		Lemons give us an important vitamin. Is it A, B or C?	*Vitamin C*
15		What is smog?	*A mixture of smoke and fog*

Quiz 80
Question 10

Quiz 80
Question 11

Quiz 80 Level 3

Questions

Answers

#		Question	Answer
1		Which Italian traveller wrote a famous account of life in the Far East?	*Marco Polo*
2		What is an alloy?	*A mixture of two or more metals*
3		Who wrote the *Alice in Wonderland* stories?	*Lewis Carroll*
4		What is an invertebrate?	*An animal that lacks a backbone*
5		What is the smallest piece of a substance that can exist on its own?	*A molecule*
6		Was Leonardo da Vinci a general, a politician or an artist?	*A great Italian artist*
7		In which sport would you use a foil?	*Fencing*
8		What does a marine biologist study?	*Sea life*
9		What is the capital of Wales?	*Cardiff*
10		Who was known as the Lady of the Lamp?	*Florence Nightingale*
11		Is a tomato a fruit or a vegetable?	*A fruit (it has seeds)*
12		What is 10 percent of 80?	*8*
13		Which river flows through London?	*River Thames*
14		Who did Wendy Darling make friends with?	*Peter Pan*
15		What is a young deer called?	*A fawn*

Quiz 79
Question 1

Quiz 79
Question 12

Quiz 81 Level 3

Questions

Answers

1		Where is the Great Barrier Reef?	*Off the north-eastern coast of Australia*
2		What is the name for a picture or design made up of many small pieces of stone or tile?	*A mosaic*
3		Who led the Russian Revolution in 1917 and became the first leader of communist Russia?	*Lenin*
4		In which sport would you use a number 5 iron?	*Golf*
5		Which planet is named after the goddess of love?	*Venus*
6		Where is the world's largest rainforest?	*The Amazon basin in South America*
7		What does a television aerial do?	*Collects television signals*
8		What are stigma, sepals, and anthers part of?	*Flowers*
9		Which scientist thought of gravity when he saw an apple fall?	*Sir Isaac Newton*
10		How many spots on a dice?	*21*
11		Who founded the Boy Scouts?	*Sir Robert Baden-Powell*
12		What does *never say die* mean?	*Never give up hope*
13		What is the name for an animal that feeds on refuse or the flesh of dead animals?	*A scavenger*
14		Where would you find a delta?	*At the mouth of a river*
15		What is a female lion called?	*A lioness*

Quiz 82
Question 3

Quiz 82
Question 9

Quiz 82
Question 12

Quiz 82 Level 3

Questions | ## Answers

#		Question	Answer
1		What is a dictator?	*A ruler who has total power*
2		In which war was the Battle of the Somme?	*World War I*
3		What plant that has white berries can you kiss under at Christmas?	*Mistletoe*
4		In which continent are the Andes Mountains?	*South America*
5		Which was London's first bridge across the Thames?	*London Bridge*
6		Do seaweeds have roots?	*No (they cling to stones, shells, etc)*
7		What is a planet?	*A large mass that orbits a star*
8		Which French military leader is usually shown with one hand inside his coat?	*Napoleon Bonaparte*
9		Can the kiwi bird fly?	*No*
10		What is the name for a space which is completely empty of air and everything else?	*A vacuum*
11		Which is higher: a baritone or a tenor?	*A tenor*
12		What did Thomas Edison invent to help us move on from gaslight?	*The light bulb*
13		Which country did England fight in the Hundred Years War?	*France*
14		How many sides has a parallelogram?	*4*
15		Which river flows through Liverpool?	*River Mersey*

Quiz 81
Question 11

Quiz 81
Question 10

Quiz 83 Level 3

Questions

Answers

		Questions	Answers
1		Which international organization was founded to care for soldiers wounded in war?	*The Red Cross*
2		What does *beauty is skin deep* mean?	*You can't judge things by appearance*
3		Loggerhead and snapping are types of what?	*Turtles*
4		Which country's flag has a white cross?	*Switzerland*
5		What is the study of acoustics?	*The study of sound*
6		Which countries make up the Iberian Peninsula?	*Spain and Portugal*
7		Where does cork come from?	*From the bark of a tree (the cork oak)*
8		What is the main difference between algebra and arithmetic?	*Algebra uses letters to stand for numbers*
9		In which war was the Battle of Gettysburg fought?	*The American Civil War*
10		Which European country has borders with France, Germany, Austria and Italy?	*Switzerland*
11		What are the Common Blue, Peacock, and Swallowtail?	*Types of butterfly*
12		What does VE Day stand for?	*Victory in Europe Day*
13		A diamond is a crystal. True or false?	*True*
14		Who was the first person to reach the South Pole?	*Roald Amundsen*
15		What is the name of the person who directs an orchestra?	*The conductor*

Quiz 84
Question 10

Quiz 84
Question 12

Quiz 84 Level 3

Questions

Answers

		Question	Answer
1		Which painter cut off his own ear?	*Vincent Van Gogh*
2		To which country do Majorca and Minorca belong?	*Spain*
3		What is the word *bus* short for?	*Omnibus*
4		Which creatures did St Patrick drive out of Ireland?	*Snakes*
5		Which continent are the islands of the the Caribbean in?	*North America*
6		Which ship brought the first pilgrims from England to America?	*The Mayflower*
7		How many degrees in a circle?	*360*
8		Which marquess drew up a set of rules for boxing?	*The Marquess of Queensberry*
9		Which is the largest country in South America?	*Brazil, by far*
10		Which American president said *read my lips*?	*George Bush*
11		What is the name for the loosely draped tunic worn by the Romans?	*The toga*
12		What are Jerseys, Herefords, and Shorthorns?	*They are breeds of cattle*
13		Which woman scientist won two Nobel Prizes?	*Marie Curie (in 1903 and 1911)*
14		How do Americans spell *centre*?	*Center*
15		What is the smallest part of a substance?	*An atom*

Quiz 83
Question 6

Quiz 83
Question 14

Quiz 85 Level 3

Questions

Answers

		Questions	Answers
1		In which city is the Arc de Triomphe?	*Paris*
2		What are Mandarins, Mallards, and Eiders?	*Types of duck*
3		Who started the Free French Movement in Britain during World War II?	*General De Gaulle*
4		What is the name of the tube which takes food from your mouth to your stomach?	*The oesophagus or gullet*
5		Who wrote a book called *On the Origin of Species*?	*Charles Darwin*
6		What is the Earth's solid outer layer called?	*The crust*
7		Two of the Brontë sisters were Charlotte and Anne. Who was the third?	*Emily*
8		Which composer continued to compose great music when he was totally deaf?	*Ludwig van Beethoven*
9		How many sides has a hexagon?	*6*
10		Which is the largest city in Africa?	*Cairo*
11		Which London bridge opens to let ships through?	*Tower Bridge*
12		What English word is made from the words for two Greek letters, *alpha* and *beta*?	*Alphabet*
13		What is a cosmonaut?	*A Russian astronaut*
14		What do butterflies use their antennae for?	*To smell*
15		How did Joan of Arc die?	*She was burnt at the stake*

Quiz 86
Question 6

Quiz 86
Question 8

Quiz 86 Level 3

Questions

#		Question	Answer
1		Which Christian church has most members?	The Roman Catholic
2		What is the capital of Sri Lanka?	Colombo
3		How many degress are there in a right angle?	90 degrees
4		Who flew the first powered aeroplane?	The Wright brothers
5		Which centre of film-making is in Los Angeles?	Hollywood
6		Who was president of the United States during the American Civil War?	Abraham Lincoln
7		What are layers of coal called?	Seams
8		Buff Orpingtons, Leghorns, Rhode Island Reds are all types of what?	Chickens
9		What are crabs, lobsters, and prawns?	They are shellfish (crustaceans)
10		Which unit of measurement uses the distance light travels in one year – 9,470,000,000,000 km?	A light-year
11		Who in 1961 was the first person to travel into space?	The Russian Yuri Gagarin
12		Complete the title of this book by C.S. Lewis: *The Lion, the Witch and the ...*	Wardrobe
13		How many English kings have been called Henry?	8
14		How do grasshoppers make a noise?	By rubbing their back legs together
15		What does *armistice* mean?	An end to fighting

Answers

Quiz 85
Question 2

Quiz 85
Question 8

Quiz 87 Level 3

Questions

		Questions	Answers
1		In which city is Lansdowne Road rugby ground?	*Dublin*
2		How far is Dover from Calais?	*22 miles (35 km)*
3		Which part of an egg is used to make mayonnaise?	*The yolk*
4		When archaeologists dig a site, what is it called?	*An excavation*
5		How many seconds are there in an hour?	*3,600*
6		What is an accurate seagoing clock called?	*A chronometer*
7		In which country are Rio de Janeiro and São Paulo?	*Brazil*
8		Which great Austrian composer wrote over 600 pieces of music, including many famous operas?	*Wolfgang Armadeus Mozart*
9		Which is the second heaviest land animal?	*The hippopotamus*
10		What is the capital of Hungary?	*Budapest*
11		Who was the famous leader of the Huns?	*Attila*
12		Are mammals warm- or cold-blooded?	*Warm-blooded*
13		Which American civil rights leader was assassinated in 1968?	*Martin Luther King*
14		Which four-sided shape has equal sides and equal angles?	*A square*
15		What does *allegiance* mean?	*Loyalty*

Quiz 88
Question 10

Quiz 88
Question 11

Quiz 88 Level 3

Questions

Answers

		Questions	Answers
1		Which country has borders with France, Germany and Holland?	*Belgium*
2		Which soft-bodied group of animals includes snails, slugs, oysters, and octopuses?	*Molluscs*
3		In which ocean is the island of Mauritius?	*The Indian Ocean*
4		What does *sarcastic* mean?	*Mocking and scornful*
5		In which city are the main administrative offices of the European Union?	*Brussels*
6		What is the name of the disorder of the blood caused by having too few red blood cells?	*Anaemia*
7		Bees don't have to learn to sting; they do it by what?	*Instinct*
8		Which country invaded Kuwait in 1990?	*Iraq*
9		On which day is American Independence Day?	*July 4*
10		Which empire specialized in building straight roads and bridges?	*The Roman*
11		What is an anemometer?	*A wind-gauge*
12		What is the capital of Mexico?	*Mexico City*
13		Who were known as Tommies?	*British soldiers (in World War I)*
14		For what is Gregor Mendel famous?	*For his work on heredity*
15		What do you call the coat of a sheep?	*Fleece*

Quiz 87
Question 3

Quiz 89 Level 3

Questions

Answers

#	Question	Answer
1	Is it true that water expands (grows bigger) as it freezes?	*Yes*
2	Which age followed the Stone Age?	*The Bronze Age*
3	Which religion celebrates Chanukah for eight days each December?	*The Jewish religion*
4	Where would you find a ligament?	*In a joint*
5	Which country has a House of Representatives and a Senate?	*The USA*
6	Which western European nation has the largest population?	*Germany (about 80 million people)*
7	Which river flows through Vienna?	*The Danube*
8	Who died in St Helena?	*Napoleon in 1821*
9	One third is approximately which decimal fraction?	*0.333*
10	Through which organs do whales breathe?	*Lungs*
11	Which insect has larva called daphnia?	*Dragonfly*
12	Which armoured fighting vehicle runs on tracks?	*The tank*
13	Who did Dr Jekyll change into?	*Edward Hyde*
14	What is the Irish name for Ireland?	*Eire*
15	What is a Chevrolet?	*A type of car*

Quiz 90
Question 12

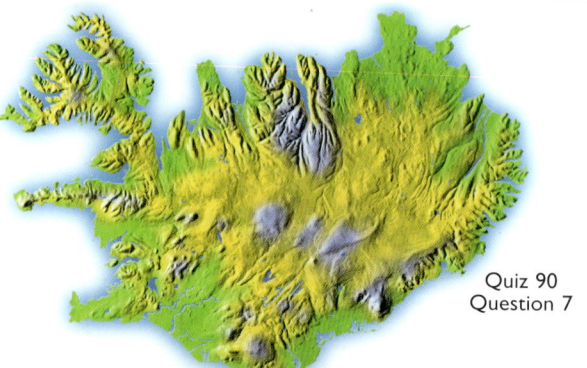

Quiz 90
Question 7

Quiz 90
Question 2

Quiz 90 Level 3

Questions

Answers

		Questions	Answers
1		What is the name for the large flat teeth at the back of the mouth used for grinding food?	*The molars*
2		His thoughts were published in a little red book. Who was he?	*Chairman Mao*
3		There are two kinds of electric current. One is direct current or DC, what is the other?	*Alternating current or AC*
4		How old is the Earth — 3 billion, 3.5 billion, 4 billion, or 4.5 billion years?	*About 4.5 billion years old*
5		What is the currency of Greece?	*The drachma*
6		Which domestic animal is sacred to the Hindus?	*The cow*
7		Reykjavik is the capital of which country?	*Iceland*
8		What is the Universe?	*All of space and everything in it*
9		What is a male pig called?	*A boar*
10		What was the name of Nelson's flagship at the Battle of Trafalgar?	*The Victory*
11		Who was Australopithecus?	*A form of ancient man*
12		How many eyes did the Cyclops have?	*1*
13		Which class of creatures contains more than two-thirds of all known species?	*Insects*
14		Frogs can breathe air through their skins. True or false?	*True*
15		What is the opposite of *loyalty*?	*Disloyalty*

Quiz 89
Question 13

Quiz 89
Question 11

Quiz 89
Question 12

Quiz 91 Level 3

Questions

Answers

#	Question	Answer
1	What colour are pistachio nuts?	*Green*
2	What do you call people who have no permanent home and move about in search of pasture?	*Nomads*
3	Which country is made up of two main islands, North Island and South Island?	*New Zealand*
4	What is an air-breathing gastropod mollusc, with a spiral shell better known as?	*A snail*
5	Which wood is used to make cricket bats?	*Willow*
6	What are your canine teeth?	*The pointed teeth, or eye teeth*
7	How many sides are there in a quadrilateral?	*4 sides*
8	Where does the Sun set?	*In the west*
9	What are chickens, ducks, geese, partridges, and pheasants?	*They are all poultry*
10	What word means *to put off until another time*?	*Postpone*
11	What collapsed in the Wall Street Crash?	*The US stock market*
12	What are conduction, convection, and radiation?	*They are three ways in which heat travels*
13	Of which country is Colonel Qaddafi the head?	*Libya*
14	What was the Yorkish symbol in the War of the Roses?	*A white rose*
15	The height of a mountain is measured from what base?	*Sea level*

Quiz 92
Question 2

Quiz 92 Level 3

Questions

Answers

		Question	Answer
1		What cause the common cold?	*Viruses*
2		What were the pyramids in ancient Egypt used for?	*Royal tombs*
3		To what group of animals do rats belong?	*Rodents*
4		Which sport do we associate with Steffi Graf?	*Tennis*
5		What is another name for Northern Ireland?	*Ulster*
6		What is a part of the circumference of a circle called?	*An arc*
7		J.M.W. Turner was what?	*An English painter*
8		What is the spiral part of a screw called?	*The thread*
9		Which soft-bodied sea creature looks like a flower?	*The sea anemone*
10		St Petersburg was renamed Leningrad. What is it called now?	*St Petersburg*
11		How many lives are cats said to have?	*9*
12		From which plant is linen made?	*Flax*
13		What destroyed Nagasaki in World War II?	*An atom bomb*
14		What does the abbreviation PTO mean?	*Please turn over*
15		Who were Virgil, Horace, and Ovid?	*Roman poets*

Quiz 91
Question 3

Quiz 91
Question 4

Quiz 93 Level 3

Questions

Answers

		Questions	Answers
1		Who composed the ballets *Swan Lake*, *The Nutcracker* and *The Sleeping Beauty*?	*Tchaikovsky*
2		What is a fandango?	*A Spanish dance*
3		Where are the Solomon Islands?	*In the Pacific Ocean*
4		Ginger, cloves, pepper and nutmeg are all what?	*Spices*
5		Alfred Nobel who donated the Nobel Prizes made his fortune from what?	*Explosives*
6		How do Americans spell *colour*?	*Color*
7		Where could you look for starfish, lugworms, razor shells, and cockles?	*On sandy or muddy beaches*
8		Where was William Shakespeare born?	*In Stratford-upon-Avon*
9		A dogfish is a small what?	*A small shark*
10		Which of the following countries are monarchies: Denmark, Norway, Sweden?	*All of them*
11		What are bakelite and celluloid?	*Early plastics*
12		Which is the leading French-speaking province of Canada?	*Quebec*
13		What are the chances of throwing two heads if you toss a coin twice?	*1 in 4*
14		What does Saturday's child do?	*Works hard for a living*
15		What is seven eighths of 56?	*49*

Quiz 94
Question 5

Quiz 94
Question 11

Quiz 94 Level 3

Questions

Answers

		Questions	Answers
1		Which science deals with heat, light, sound, electricity and mechanics?	*Physics*
2		What musical instrument developed from virginals and harpsichords?	*The piano*
3		Which animal can be eaten for meat, and whose fat, skin and hair give lard, leather and brushes?	*The pig*
4		How many notes are there in an octave?	*8*
5		Which Australian animal is a mammal which lays eggs, but feeds its young on its milk?	*The platypus*
6		Which country do the Azores and Madeira islands belong to?	*Portugal*
7		What is the common name for cups, saucers, tiles and bricks?	*Pottery*
8		In grammar, what kind of words are *he*, *she*, *it*, *they*?	*Pronouns*
9		What is the name for a star that gives out regular pulses of radio waves?	*A pulsar*
10		Which disease is spread by the bite of infected dogs or wild animals?	*Rabies*
11		Which English sailor, soldier and explorer brought tobacco to Europe from America?	*Sir Walter Raleigh*
12		Which sea separates northeast Africa from Arabia?	*The Red Sea*
13		What striped animal gave its name to a pedestrian crossing?	*The zebra*
14		Which long river rises in Switzerland, flows through Germany to Holland and the North Sea?	*The Rhine*
15		Complete the phrase: *as fresh as a ....*	*Daisy*

Quiz 93
Question 4

Quiz 93
Question 9

Quiz 95 Level 3

Questions

		Answers
1	Who was Paul Cezanne?	A famous French painter
2	Which country produces the most gold?	South Africa
3	What is eaten with cream at Wimbledon?	Strawberries
4	What do daffodils, bluebells and crocuses have in common?	They all grow from bulbs
5	Methane is the main part of which widely used fuel?	Natural gas
6	Where was the Biosphere 2 experiment?	Arizona
7	What is the capital of Kenya?	Nairobi
8	Who was Mowgli?	The boy (in 'Jungle Book')
9	On which Japanese city was the first atomic bomb dropped?	Hiroshima
10	How many players are there in a hockey team?	11
11	Who wrote *Mein Kampf*?	Adolf Hitler
12	Which of coal and oil is a fossil fuel?	They both are fossil fuels
13	Which Australian state is an island?	Tasmania
14	What is a terrapin?	A freshwater turtle
15	What is a substance called that gives off heat when it burns?	A fuel

Quiz 96
Question 2

Quiz 96
Question 14

Quiz 96
Question 11

Quiz 96 Level 3

Questions

Answers

1	When does Lent end?	*On Easter Sunday*
2	Which insect makes its nest from chewed up mud or wood?	*The wasp*
3	The Adriatic and Aegean Seas are part of which sea?	*The Mediterranean*
4	Which organs remove waste products from the blood?	*The kidneys*
5	Seoul is the capital of which Korea?	*South Korea*
6	What is the masculine of mare?	*Stallion*
7	What is another name for ground nuts?	*Peanuts*
8	Which singer was known as *The King*?	*Elvis Presley*
9	Which English scientist put forward the law of gravity?	*Isaac Newton*
10	From which tree do we get syrup?	*The sugar maple*
11	Which is the savage fish from South America which attacks the flesh of other fish and mammals?	*The piranha*
12	Which black birds live in the Tower of London?	*Ravens*
13	Which vitamin are oranges full of?	*Vitamin C*
14	What is the name for the fibrous tissue which joins a muscle to a bone?	*A tendon*
15	What does *frivolous* mean?	*Silly, not useful*

Quiz 95
Question 14

Quiz 95
Question 11

Quiz 97 Level 3

Questions

Answers

		Question	Answer
1		In which country is the Tigris River?	*Iraq*
2		Who had a magic lamp?	*Aladdin*
3		What is a migraine?	*A severe prolonged headache*
4		What is silent acting called?	*Mime*
5		The Missouri is a tributary of which river?	*The Mississippi*
6		Who lived in Holyrood Palace?	*Scottish kings and queens*
7		Which American spacecraft made its first flight in 1981?	*The Shuttle*
8		What is the capital of Pakistan?	*Islamabad*
9		What is the name of an automatic device for controlling temperature?	*A thermostat*
10		George V, Edward VIII, George VI and Elizabeth II are of which royal house?	*The House of Windsor*
11		What is another name for a puma?	*A cougar*
12		British sailors in the Navy receive a a daily ration of rum. True or false?	*False (it was stopped in 1970)*
13		Which prehistoric cat-like animal had two canine teeth about 20cm long?	*The sabre-toothed tiger*
14		Which warrior caste of Japan followed a strict code of behaviour?	*The Samurai*
15		What does it mean to be *cut to the quick*? Quiz 98 Question 13	*To be deeply hurt*

Quiz 98 Level 3

	Questions	Answers
1	Who started cubism and is considered the most famous modern painter?	*Pablo Picasso*
2	What was another name for the Plague?	*The Black Death*
3	Which nutritional food group are milk, meat, eggs, fish and nuts rich in?	*Protein*
4	The Red Sea is a branch of which ocean?	*The Indian Ocean*
5	What is the capital of Romania?	*Bucharest*
6	What happens if iron and steel are left exposed to air and moisture?	*They rust*
7	Which American city is famous for gambling?	*Las Vegas*
8	Who wrote *Treasure Island*?	*Robert Louis Stevenson*
9	Which sea mammal looks like a seal, but has fur on its body, and, unlike the seal, has ears?	*The sea lion*
10	What is the opposite of *legal*?	*Illegal*
11	Which worldwide disease has been wiped out by vaccination?	*Smallpox*
12	General Franco was dictator of which country?	*Spain*
13	The Cavaliers and Roundheads were opponents in which war?	*The English Civil War*
14	Which country's flag shows a red maple leaf?	*Canada*
15	What is a joey?	*A newborn kangaroo*

Quiz 97
Question 7

Quiz 99 Level 3

Questions

Answers

1	What kind of flag is waved to show the winner of a motor race?	*A black and white chequered flag*
2	Which American state is called the *Lone Star State*?	*Texas*
3	Who wrote the *Just So Stories*?	*Rudyard Kipling*
4	In swimming pools, which chemical is added to water to kill germs?	*Chlorine*
5	Which American president was given the sack?	*Richard Nixon*
6	Which vegetable makes you cry?	*The onion*
7	What is the name for a substance which makes a person immune to a certain disease?	*A vaccine*
8	Where is Ecuador?	*In northwestern South America*
9	What does *making a mountain out of a molehill* mean?	*Exaggerating a problem*
10	Who was the first American president to be assassinated?	*Abraham Lincoln*
11	Which South American animal is used as a pack horse by the people of the Andes?	*The llama*
12	Which river do Hindus consider sacred?	*The Ganges*
13	What is an expert judge, especially of food and drink called?	*A connoisseur*
14	What do you call a male goose?	*A gander*
15	Which instrument did Chopin play?	*The piano*

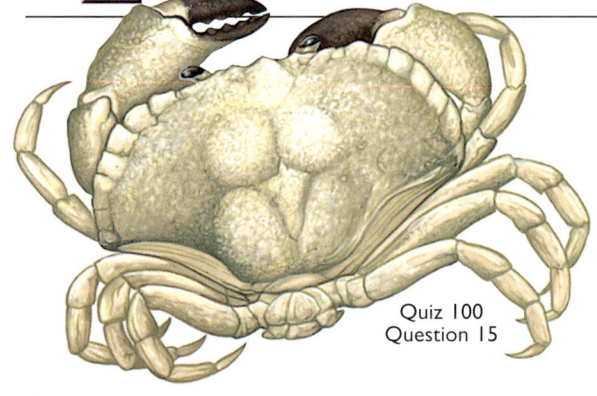

Quiz 100
Question 15

Quiz 100
Question 9

Quiz 100 Level 3

Questions

Answers

		Question	Answer
1		Lhasa is the capital of which country?	*Tibet*
2		Who flew the *Spirit of St Louis* across the Atlantic?	*Charles Lindbergh*
3		Which sea did Moses cross with the Israelites?	*The Red Sea*
4		A gun that fires a bullet along a spirally grooved barrel is called ..?	*A rifle*
5		What is the name of the largest planet in the Solar System?	*Jupiter*
6		Who was the Soviet communist leader during World War II?	*Joseph Stalin*
7		Who is the messenger of love in Roman myths?	*Cupid with his bow and arrow*
8		Of which family was Bonnie Prince Charlie?	*The Stuarts*
9		Who was the mythological figure with a human head and lion's body?	*The sphinx*
10		Mars was the Roman god of what?	*War*
11		What is the weak mixture of acetic acid and water, used for flavouring food and for pickling?	*Vinegar*
12		Which is the most commonly used letter in the English alphabet?	*The letter E*
13		The name of which animal means *a thousand legs*?	*The millipede*
14		What is the opposite of *obedient*?	*Disobedient*
15		How many legs has a crab?	*10*

Quiz 99
Question 3

Quiz 99
Question 6

Quiz 101 Level 3

Questions

1		What is the capital of New South Wales, Australia?	
2		What is a thrombosis?	
3		What is fishing with a large bag-shaped net dragged along the bottom of the sea called?	
4		What metal is mainly used to fuel nuclear reactors?	
5		Which material is mostly used for making transistors?	
6		What kind of stories did Jules Verne and H.G. Wells write?	
7		What are the epidermis and the dermis?	Quiz 26 Question 8
8		What is the modern name for the game Tiddlywinks?	
9		Where is your thyroid?	
10		What did Laszlo Biro invent?	
11		What is the name for animals that eat only plants?	
12		What is Easter Island famous for?	
13		What is similar to a porpoise, but has a beak-like snout and swims farther from land?	
14		Who ordered the execution of Mary Queen of Scots?	
15		Who was Tarzan's girlfriend?	

Answers

1. Sydney
2. A clot in a blood vessel
3. Trawling
4. Uranium
5. Silicon
6. Science fiction
7. Layers of the skin
8. Pogs
9. In your neck
10. The ballpoint pen
11. Herbivores
12. Its strange stone figures
13. A dolphin
14. Queen Elizabeth I
15. Jane

Quiz 102 Question 15

Quiz 102 Question 1

Quiz 102 Level 3

Questions / Answers

	Questions	Answers
1	In what country is parliament called Congress?	*The USA*
2	Where would you find a proton?	*At the centre of an atom*
3	What is the main product of Kuwait?	*Oil*
4	Which region includes parts of Norway, Sweden, Finland and Russia?	*Lapland*
5	What is a loop of electrical conductors called?	*An electrical circuit*
6	What is the name of food prepared according to Jewish law?	*Kosher*
7	What is particularly prominent in the Proboscis monkey?	*Its nose*
8	What country's national symbol is the harp?	*Ireland*
9	How many players are there in a netball team?	*7*
10	What is a smaller form of kangaroo usually called?	*A wallaby*
11	Where did Drake's famous game of bowls take place?	*Plymouth Hoe*
12	Where is the seat of government of the Netherlands?	*The Hague*
13	Who was Henry VIII's first queen?	*Catherine of Aragon*
14	In which book did Long John Silver feature?	*'Treasure Island'*
15	What are felines?	*Cats*

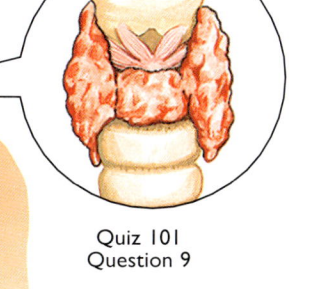

Quiz 101
Question 9

Quiz 101
Question 12

Quiz 103 Level 3

Questions

Answers

#		Question	Answer
1		Who was Plato?	*A famous Greek philosopher*
2		Which is the largest building on the Acropolis in Athens?	*The Parthenon*
3		Which sweet substance is used in the diet of diabetics and slimmers?	*Saccharin*
4		The sap of which tree is called latex?	*The rubber tree*
5		How does sound reach our ears?	*It is carried by vibrations*
6		What is the average thickness of the Antarctic ice – 20 m, 200 m, or 2,000 m?	*2,000 m*
7		Who was the first pope?	*St Peter*
8		What is a table tennis ball made of?	*Celluloid*
9		What do we mean when we say: *Don't put all your eggs in one basket*?	*Don't rely on one thing*
10		In which country is Monument Valley?	*The USA*
11		What is the longest river in Ireland?	*The Shannon*
12		Who designed St Paul's Cathedral in London?	*Sir Christopher Wren*
13		Who was Ned Kelly?	*An Australian outlaw*
14		What kind of creature is an avocet?	*A wading bird*
15		Which American city is famous for its cable cars?	*San Francisco*

Quiz 104
Question 7

Quiz 104
Question 2

Quiz 104 Level 3

	Questions	Answers
1	What is 100 degrees centigrade on the Fahrenheit scale?	*212 degrees*
2	What is the architectural name for a grotesque carved head designed to catch rainwater?	*A gargoyle*
3	What was the name of the census carried out in England by William the Conqueror?	*The Domesday Book*
4	What is a digital image generated from an equation called?	*A fractal*
5	In which direction would you look for the Sun at midday in the Southern hemisphere?	*North*
6	On what date is St Patrick's Day?	*March 17*
7	What are these all varieties of: broccoli, brussel sprouts and cauliflower?	*Cabbage*
8	Which poet wrote *The Wreck of the Hesperus* and *The Song of Hiawatha*?	*Longfellow*
9	What is the capital of Chile?	*Santiago*
10	Hades was the Greek god of what?	*The dead*
11	What is the measurement and mapping of the Earth's surface called?	*Surveying*
12	What do you use to turn sound waves into small electric currents so they can be recorded?	*A microphone*
13	What does *steal a march* on someone mean?	*Gain advantage*
14	Where are a grasshopper's ears?	*In its knees*
15	What are vertebrae?	*Bones in your backbone*

Quiz 103
Question 10

Quiz 105 Level 3

Questions

Answers

		Question	Answer
1		Manila is the chief port and capital of which country?	*The Philippines*
2		Who discovered penicillin?	*Alexander Fleming*
3		When is a person illiterate?	*When they can't read or write*
4		Which Dutch painter produced about 60 self-portraits and painted *The Night Watch*?	*Rembrandt*
5		Which is the largest member of the cat family?	*The Siberian tiger*
6		Who wrote *Waverley*, *Rob Roy* and *Heart of Midlothian*?	*Walter Scott*
7		What is the capital of Finland?	*Helsinki*
8		How many Georges have been king?	*6*
9		What kind of boat skims across the surface of the water on underwater wings?	*A hydrofoil*
10		The trunk of which tree swells in wet weather and shrinks in dry weather?	*The baobab tree*
11		What is two thirds written as a decimal?	*0.666 repeating (0.67)*
12		What do doctors use to inject drugs into the body?	*A syringe*
13		What kind of stone did early people use to make tools and weapons?	*Flint*
14		What are the largest pieces of land on Earth called?	*Continents*
15		Which metal makes the strongest magnets?	*Iron*

Quiz 106
Question 15

Quiz 106
Question 7

Quiz 106 Level 3

Questions

Answers

#	Question	Answer
1	How do pythons and anacondas kill their prey?	By squeezing and suffocating it
2	What part of the body does a chiropodist treat?	The feet
3	In which city is the Kremlin?	Moscow
4	Did dinosaurs lay eggs?	Yes, like all reptiles
5	Who was the first European to explore the coasts of Australia and New Zealand?	Captain James Cook
6	What type of courts is Wimbledon famous for?	Grass courts
7	What is the name for all the bodies that orbit the Sun and the Sun itself?	The Solar System
8	What is the name of a word made by re-arranging the letters of another word?	Anagram
9	What is the name for the stone at the top of an arch which locks the whole arch together?	The keystone
10	Who wrote *The Ugly Duckling*?	Hans Christian Andersen
11	In which country is the huge rock known as Uluru?	Australia
12	Which is the smallest prime number?	1
13	Which US president had talks with the Soviet Union which led to the end of the Cold War?	Ronald Reagan
14	Why does the Sun look the same size as the Moon although it is many millions times bigger?	Because it is much farther away
15	Where are the Northwest Territories?	Canada

Quiz 105
Question 9

Quiz 105
Question 5

Quiz 107 Level 3

Questions

Answers

		Questions	Answers
1		Which kind of heavenly body is made of very hot gas and gives out heat and light?	*A star*
2		Who is head of the Church of England?	*The king or queen of Great Britain*
3		What is the name for a creature that eats all kinds of food, both plants and animals?	*An omnivore*
4		What does humidity measure?	*The amount of water in the air*
5		In which country is Harvard University?	*The USA*
6		How many pairs of wings does a fly have?	*2*
7		What is another name for a capsicum?	*A pepper*
8		How did Stegosaurus defend itself?	*It had thick, bony plates, like armour*
9		Which Indian city produces more films than Hollywood?	*Bombay*
10		Which country has the second largest population in the world?	*India*
11		Where does the jaguar live?	*In the forests of South America*
12		What is a kibbutz?	*A collective farm in Israel*
13		Which country is Beirut the capital of?	*The Lebanon*
14		The people of which ancient civilization spilt a drop of blood every morning to please their gods?	*The Aztecs*
15		What is the square of 11?	*121*

Quiz 108
Question 14

Quiz 108
Question 8

Quiz 108 Level 3

Questions

Answers

	Questions	Answers
1	Does Mars have any moons?	*Yes (2 – Deimos and Phobos)*
2	What lies under the ice at the North Pole?	*Sea*
3	What is a *stage whisper*?	*One that everyone can hear*
4	Which grassland animal digs interlinking underground burrows?	*The prairie dog*
5	Where is the Cape of Good Hope?	*At the southern tip of Africa*
6	Who wrote *Pilgrim's Progress*?	*John Bunyan*
7	How did Marie Antoinette die during the French Revolution?	*She was executed*
8	Who was Norma Jean?	*Marilyn Monroe*
9	Which country was ruled by tsars?	*Russia*
10	What do whales feed their young on?	*Milk (they are mammals)*
11	Which king signed the Magna Carta?	*King John*
12	Of which religion is the *Torah* the holy book?	*Judaism*
13	Which is the only metal that is liquid at room temperature?	*Mercury*
14	Doric, Ionic and Corinthian are all what?	*Orders of architecture*
15	What is the capital of Iraq?	*Baghdad*

Quiz 107
Question 6

Quiz 107
Question 7

Quiz 109 Level 3

Questions

Answers

		Question	Answer
1		Which sea creatures swim by squirting out water through a tube?	*Squids and octopuses*
2		In which game was the phrase *hat trick* first used?	*Cricket*
3		Who wrote a book about Jemima Puddleduck?	*Beatrix Potter*
4		Who landed in Britain in 55 BC?	*Julius Caesar*
5		How many wings has a dragonfly?	*4*
6		Which sea is really the world's largest lake?	*The Caspian Sea*
7		Who is the American state of Virginia named after?	*Queen Elizabeth I, the Virgin Queen*
8		How many square metres are there in a hectare?	*10,000*
9		What was the name of the fairy in *Peter Pan*?	*Tinkerbell*
10		What is the only food of vampire bats?	*Blood*
11		Which is the largest island in the Caribbean Sea?	*Cuba*
12		Athletes sometimes damage their achilles tendon. Where is it?	*At the back of the heel*
13		What is the more common name for Poseidon, the Greek god of the sea?	*Neptune*
14		What is the name for an area in space which sucks everything into itself, even light?	*A black hole*
15		Which river runs through Newcastle?	*The Tyne*

Quiz 110
Question 8

Quiz 110 Level 3

Questions

Answers

		Questions	Answers
1		What force holds the Earth in its path around the Sun?	*Gravity*
2		Were there any people around when the dinosaurs lived?	*No*
3		What sort of person is called *a tower of strength*?	*A reliable, comforting person*
4		What is bauxite used for? Quiz 109 Question 1	*Making aluminium*
5		How do camels avoid sinking into the sand?	*They have large feet*
6		What is the name of the headquarters of the United States armed forces?	*The Pentagon*
7		Where did a great fire take place in 1666?	*In London*
8		Which ocean liner was said to be unsinkable but sank on its first voyage?	*The Titanic*
9		Which city is said to be built on seven hills?	*Rome*
10		What is the name for the process which turns animals skins into leather?	*Tanning*
12		What type of trees make up the largest forest in the world?	*Conifers*
11		What is a female fox called?	*Vixen*
13		What is the female of hero?	*Heroine*
14		Of which country is Kampala the capital?	*Uganda*
15		Name a disease spread by some kinds of mosquito.	*Malaria and yellow fever*

Quiz 109
Question 13

Quiz 111 Level 3

Questions | Answers

#	Question	Answer
1	Which city is called The Big Apple?	*New York*
2	Where are the bones the tibia, the fibula and the femur?	*In your leg*
3	How can you tell the age of a felled tree?	*By counting the rings on its stump*
4	Which black powder is made from saltpetre, sulphur and carbon?	*Gunpowder*
5	When do married people celebrate their golden wedding?	*On their 50th wedding anniversary*
6	What is a macaw?	*A brightly coloured parrot*
7	What word describes creatures that come out at night?	*Nocturnal*
8	Where is the earthquake danger zone known as the San Andreas Fault?	*California*
9	In which country is the Black Forest?	*Germany*
10	In which religion do boys have a Barmitzvah?	*Judaism*
11	What powered Stephenson's *Rocket*?	*Steam*
12	Which American flew a kite in a thunderstorm to prove that lightning was electricity?	*Benjamin Franklin*
13	Cereals, such as wheat, oats and rice, are cultivated what?	*Grasses*
14	Who was Cicero?	*A famous Roman orator*
15	Which river is Glasgow built on?	*The Clyde*

Quiz 112
Question 9

Quiz 112
Question 1

Quiz 112 Level 3

Questions

Answers

		Questions	Answers
1		Which Australian bird is also called the laughing jackass?	*The kookaburra*
2		Which sport uses the smaller ball, tennis or squash?	*Squash*
3		What is the name of the famous statue of the goddess Venus in the Louvre Museum in Paris?	*Venus de Milo*
4		Gandhi was given the name Mahatma. What does *Mahatma* mean?	*Great soul*
5		What is an ampersand?	*The character &*
6		What is ebony?	*A hard jet-black wood*
7		Which method of healing involves inserting needles into the body at certain points?	*Acupuncture*
8		*They jumped through the hoop.* Which is the verb in that sentence?	*Jumped*
9		Which planet is called the Ringed Planet?	*Saturn*
10		What did William Wallace and Robert the Bruce fight for about 700 years ago?	*Scotland's independence*
11		Which is the only creature that can turn its head in an almost complete circle?	*The owl*
12		For which service did press gangs recruit men in the early 19th century?	*The navy*
13		What is the name of the disorder caused by pollen from plants floating in the air?	*Hayfever*
14		What does NASA, in the USA do?	*Launches spacecraft and satellites*
15		What won't a rolling stone gather?	*Moss*

Quiz 111
Question 11

Quiz 111
Question 6

Quiz 113 Level 3

Questions

Answers

		Question	Answer
1		Which is the highest mountain in Africa?	*Mount Kilimanjaro*
2		Where does the oxygen in the air come from?	*Plants*
3		Which country did Burke and Wills explore?	*Australia*
4		What are the wild reindeer of North America called?	*Caribou*
5		What do you get if you mix zinc and copper?	*Brass*
6		What is the capital of Argentina?	*Buenos Aires*
7		What do Frederick Ashton, Marie Rambert and Margot Fonteyn have in common?	*Ballet*
8		Who wrote *The Canterbury Tales*?	*Geoffrey Chaucer*
9		What kind of creature is a Gila monster?	*A lizard*
10		What is porridge made from?	*Oats and water*
11		What is 10 percent of 65?	*6.5*
12		What is the silent letter in rhubarb?	*H*
13		Where is the Rift Valley?	*In eastern Africa*
14		What code uses short and long signals?	*Morse code*
15		Which sport has birdies, eagles and chips?	*Golf*

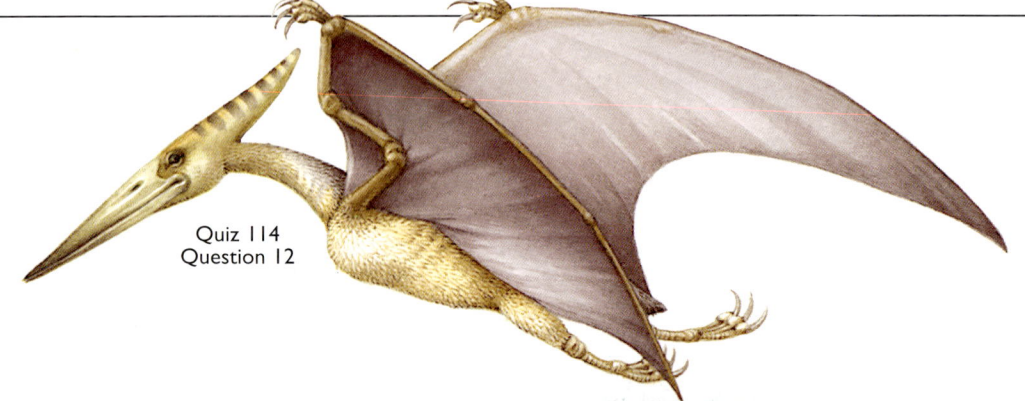

Quiz 114
Question 12

Quiz 114 Level 3

Questions

Answers

#	Question	Answer
1	How many players are there in a baseball team?	*Nine*
2	Bermuda is a colony of which country?	*Britain*
3	What is an anaesthetic used for?	*To deaden pain*
4	What is the capital city of the USA?	*Washington DC*
5	Which army destroyed the Inca empire in 1532?	*The Spanish conquistadors*
6	What are ceramics?	*Porcelain and pottery*
7	What is the name for the wearing away of the land by running water, weather, ice and wind?	*Erosion*
8	Which animal lives on the leaves of the eucalyptus tree?	*The koala*
9	Where would you see cirrocumulus?	*In the sky, it is a type of cloud*
10	Who was Emily Pankhurst?	*A famous suffragette*
11	What does a starfish do if it loses an arm?	*It grows another one*
12	Name a prehistoric flying reptile?	*Pterodactyl*
13	What are Wedgewood, Royal Doulton and Royal Worcester?	*Makes of pottery*
14	What does *play your cards close to your chest* mean?	*Not give any information away*
15	Where is Namibia?	*In southwest Africa*

Quiz 113
Question 4

Quiz 113
Question 3

Quiz 115 Level 4

Questions | Answers

#		Question	Answer
1		Which planet is usually furthest from the Sun?	*Pluto*
2		Which is the largest continent?	*Asia*
3		Which drink is made from hops?	*Beer*
4		What does a pediatric doctor specialize in?	*Children*
5		Do whales feed their young on milk?	*Yes (whales are mammals)*
6		Who was the first American president?	*George Washington*
7		Who was Robert Burns?	*A Scottish poet*
8		Would you weigh more or less on the Moon?	*Less*
9		How many continents are there?	*7*
10		What carry satellites into space?	*Rockets*
11		Do veins carry blood to or from the heart?	*To the heart*
12		Who wrote *Gulliver's Travels*?	*Jonathan Swift*
13		What are trees that produce cones called?	*Conifers*
14		Which is the world's largest island?	*Greenland*
15		What is the name of King Arthur's sword?	*Excalibur*

Quiz 116
Question 4

Quiz 116
Question 2

Quiz 116 Level 4

Questions

Answers

		Question	Answer
1		Who was shipwrecked in a land of tiny people?	*Gulliver*
2		What is a Portuguese man-o'-war?	*A kind of jellyfish*
3		Why does the Moon shine?	*Because it reflects light from the Sun*
4		Who was the Italian Fascist leader during World War II?	*Benito Mussolini*
5		What does a barometer measure?	*Air pressure*
6		In which war were tanks first used?	*World War I*
7		What is fog?	*A cloud that forms close to the ground*
8		In which sport do teams compete for the Jules Rimet cup?	*Football*
9		What is the past tense of *strike*?	*Struck*
10		Which planet is nearest to the Sun?	*Mercury*
11		Which group of plants do mushrooms, toadstools and moulds belong to?	*Fungi*
12		In which ocean is Tahiti?	*The Pacific*
13		Who invented the telephone in 1876?	*Alexander Graham Bell*
14		What movement in the USA did Martin Luther King lead?	*The Civil Rights movement*
15		What is the fiery liquid which flows from a volcano called?	*Lava*

Quiz 115
Question 10

Quiz 115
Question 14

Quiz 117 Level 4

Questions

Answers

		Question	Answer
1		What is the off-spring of a donkey and a horse?	*A mule*
2		What does *unique* mean?	*Only one of its kind*
3		What is the larval stage of the butterfly and the moth?	*The caterpillar*
4		What is two fifths of 25?	*10*
5		How many oceans are there?	*4 – Pacific, Atlantic, Indian and Arctic*
6		What does an antiseptic do?	*It kills bacteria*
7		Who took a force of elephants across the alps?	*Hannibal*
8		Which religion follows the teachings of the Koran?	*Islam*
9		Which scientist produced the Theory of Relativity?	*Albert Einstein*
10		In which war did Florence Nightingale nurse wounded soldiers?	*Crimean War*
11		What is a narrow inlet of the sea that is surrounded by mountains or hills called?	*A fiord*
12		Which language is spoken by more people than any other?	*Mandarin Chinese*
13		Who ruled England during the Commonwealth?	*Oliver Cromwell*
14		What is the name for the branch of biology that studies plants?	*Botany*
15		What does a banyan tree have lots of?	*Trunks*

Quiz 118
Question 11

Quiz 118
Question 12

Quiz 118 Level 4

Questions

Answers

		Questions	Answers
1		What crashed in the Wall Street Crash?	*The US Stock Market*
2		From which country does the flamenco dance come?	*Spain*
3		Which Arctic mammal is one of the largest land carnivores?	*Polar bear*
4		Which continents form the New World?	*North and South America*
5		Which British explorer did Roald Amundsen beat to the South Pole in 1911?	*Robert Scott*
6		What does a forensic scientist do?	*Provides technical details about a crime*
7		What does the Bayeux Tapestry show?	*The invasion of England in 1066*
8		Where is Tierra del Fuego?	*At the southern tip of South America*
9		How does a radio telescope see objects that are too dim for an ordinary telescope?	*It collects radio waves from space*
10		Which layer of special oxygen in the atmosphere blocks out dangerous radiation from the Sun?	*Ozone layer*
11		What brightly coloured parrots are found in American tropical forests?	*Macaws*
12		In the Napoleonic Wars, was Napoleon's invasion of Russia in 1812 a success?	*No, he had to retreat from Moscow*
13		Which blood-sucking worm is sometimes used by doctors?	*The leech*
14		About 80 percent of all animals are insects. True or false?	*True*
15		What was the Nazi symbol called?	*The swastika*

Quiz 117
Question 1

Quiz 117
Question 9

Quiz 119 Level 4

	Questions	Answers
1	What would you do to a pavane, a polonaise, and a polka?	*Dance*
2	Which of these foods were not rationed in Britain during World War II: potatoes, sugar, eggs?	*Potatoes*
3	In which sport would you play a chukka?	*In polo*
4	How many planets are there in the solar system?	*9*
5	What is the word for the study of plants and animals in relation to their surroundings?	*Ecology*
6	Which English settlers founded Plymouth Colony in America in 1620?	*The Pilgrim Fathers*
7	Which very large island is a self-governing part of Denmark?	*Greenland*
8	Who wrote *The Secret Garden*?	*Frances Hodgson Burnett*
9	What does an anemometer measure?	*The strength of the wind*
10	What is the name for the temperature at which a liquid changes to a solid?	*The freezing point*
11	What is the capital of Poland?	*Warsaw*
12	Who painted the famous Impressionist picture *Sunflowers*?	*Vincent Van Gogh*
13	Some animals blend in with their surroundings. What is this called?	*Camouflage*
14	Who is the patron saint of Wales?	*St David*
15	Name one of Christopher Columbus's ships?	*Santa María, Niña*

Quiz 120
Question 3

Quiz 120
Question 5

Quiz 120 Level 4

Questions

Answers

1	How many states are there in the United States?	50
2	What is the name for the group of nations, which were once part of the British Empire?	*The Commonwealth*
3	Who first climbed Mount Everest?	*Edmund Hillary and Tensing Norgay*
4	What is water made of?	*Oxygen and hydrogen*
5	Is it a frog or a toad which has dry, rough skin, covered with warts?	*A toad*
6	What is the name of the hottest place in the United States?	*Death Valley*
7	What precious substance comes from the tusks and also the horns and teeth of animals?	*Ivory*
8	What is the most powerful chess piece?	*The queen*
9	Which is the longest snake?	*The python (up to 10 m long)*
10	Which English queen ruled only for nine days?	*Lady Jane Grey*
11	Who fell asleep for 20 years in a story by the American writer Washington Irving?	*Rip Van Winkle*
12	In which year was Elizabeth II crowned?	*1952*
13	Which calculating machine uses movable beads for doing sums?	*An abacus*
14	Which Roman governor of Judaea ordered the crucifixion of Christ?	*Pontius Pilate*
15	What, in Herman Melville's novel *Moby Dick*, was Moby Dick?	*A great white whale*

Quiz 119
Question 2

Quiz 119
Question 15

Quiz 121 Level 4

	Questions	Answers
1	What is 255 divided by 5?	*51*
2	What is the name for a young male horse less than four years old?	*A colt*
3	What word is used for water which does not lather easily with soap?	*Hard*
4	When we say that someone is *up a gum tree*, what do we mean?	*He or she is in difficulties*
5	Which expensive food is obtained from the eggs of a large fish called a sturgeon?	*Caviar*
6	Who has been the leader of Cuba since 1959?	*Fidel Castro*
7	What does plastic surgery do?	*It changes a person's appearance*
8	What is an oracle?	*Someone who foretells the future*
9	What is the silent letter in salmon?	*The letter l*
10	Which bird has the greatest wingspan?	*The wandering albatross*
11	Which is the biggest state in the USA?	*Alaska*
12	What is a group of lions called?	*A pride*
13	Which Roman emperor built a wall right across England?	*Emperor Hadrian*
14	What do the letters UN stand for?	*United Nations*
15	Where would you look for stalactites and stalagmites?	*In a limestone cave*

Quiz 122
Question 1

Quiz 122
Question 14

Quiz 122 Level 4

	Questions	Answers
1	Which ancient type of boat used in Wales was made from skins fixed to a wooden frame?	*Coracle*
2	What does *facsimile* mean?	*An exact copy*
3	Which alphabet begins with the letter *alpha*?	*The Greek alphabet*
4	Where are the Victoria Falls?	*On the Zambia-Zimbabwe border*
5	*Dr Livingstone, I presume.* Who said that?	*Henry Stanley*
6	Who painted the *Mona Lisa*?	*Leonardo da Vinci*
7	How many millimetres are there in 2.5 metres?	*2,500*
8	Which nut is made into butter?	*The peanut*
9	Who wrote *Huckleberry Finn*?	*Mark Twain*
10	Where is Nova Scotia?	*A province on the east coast of Canada*
11	Which nation invented fireworks?	*China*
12	What do cotton, silk, wool and flax have in common?	*They are all natural fibres*
13	What is another name for Northern Ireland?	*Ulster*
14	What would you do with claret?	*Drink it. (It's a kind of red wine)*
15	What is the boiling point of water?	*100 degrees Celsius (212 degrees F)*

Quiz 121
Question 10

Quiz 123 Level 4

Questions

Answers

#		Question	Answer
1		What is a contradiction?	*The opposite of something else*
2		How long does it take for the Moon to go round the Earth?	*Almost a month (27.33 days)*
3		Are there any cold deserts?	*Yes (including the Arctic)*
4		What was the war between the American northern and southern states (1861-1865)?	*American Civil War*
5		In which continents would you find marsupials?	*Australasia and the Americas*
6		Which great woman scientist discovered radium?	*Marie Curie*
7		Some animals journey each year to the same place to breed. What is this called?	*Migration*
8		What makes bread rise?	*Yeast*
9		What is the stratosphere?	*A layer in the atmosphere*
10		Which warm sea current crosses the Atlantic Ocean and flows up the west coast of Britain?	*The Gulf Stream*
11		What were Viking ships called?	*Longboats*
12		What are tins made of?	*Steel, coated with tin*
13		What is a pesticide?	*Chemicals which kill animal pests*
14		Who wrote *The Hobbit*?	*J.R.R. Tolkien*
15		Too much of which gas in the atmosphere causes global warming?	*Carbon dioxide*

Quiz 124
Question 9

Quiz 124 Level 4

Questions | Answers

#		Question	Answer
1		An hors d'oeuvre forms which part of a meal?	*The first course*
2		Who invented the gramophone?	*Thomas Edison*
3		Which reptiles camouflage themselves by changing colour?	*Chameleons*
4		Which domestic animal was worshipped by the ancient Egyptians?	*The cat*
5		Who wrote *Northanger Abbey*?	*Jane Austen*
6		What is the name for microscopic single-celled organisms which can cause disease?	*Bacteria*
7		Which Australian state is Melbourne the capital of?	*Victoria*
8		Which kind of animal has the most ribs?	*The snake*
9		Which eighteenth-century British explorer first landed at Botany Bay, Australia?	*Captain James Cook*
10		Mauna Kea is the tallest mountain in the world. True or false?	*True (measured from the ocean floor)*
11		Fish get oxygen from the water by breathing through what?	*Their gills*
12		What is the least number of games you would need to play to win a set in tennis?	*6*
13		How many sides does a heptagon have?	*7*
14		What does *precarious* mean?	*Not safe*
15		What disease can be caused by sunburn?	*Skin cancer*

Quiz 123
Question 4

Quiz 125 Level 4

Questions

Answers

		Questions	Answers
1		What is the longest day in the Northern hemisphere?	*June 21*
2		What is the opposite of patient?	*Impatient*
3		What is a foetus?	*An unborn baby*
4		Are bulls colour blind?	*Yes*
5		What destroyed the Roman city of Pompeii?	*A volcanic eruption*
6		Which is longer – the small intestine or the large intestine?	*The small intestine*
7		Which is the largest manmade structure on the Earth?	*The Great Wall of China*
8		Which is our nearest star?	*The Sun*
9		Which African country is Accra the capital of?	*Ghana*
10		Which word in this sentence is an adjective: *The fierce dog barked loudly*?	*Fierce*
11		What is an acute angle?	*An angle between 0 and 90 degrees*
12		Who set out in 1519 to lead the first successful expedition to sail around the world?	*Ferdinand Magellan*
13		Which reddish planet lies between Jupiter and the Earth in the solar system?	*Mars*
14		Which is the world's largest bear?	*The kodiak bear*
15		Which gases do plants absorb from the air?	*Carbon dioxide and oxygen*

Quiz 126
Question 13

Quiz 126
Question 12

Quiz 126 Level 4

Questions

Answers

#		Question	Answer
1		Where did the earliest known people live?	*In Africa (the Great Rift Valley)*
2		Where is the smallest bone in your body?	*Inside the ear*
3		Which is the biggest kind of fish?	*The whale shark*
4		Which artist painted *The Haywain* and other scenes of the English countryside?	*John Constable*
5		Which day is the longest in the Southern hemisphere?	*December 21*
6		Can fish make a noise?	*Yes some can (by grinding their teeth)*
7		Which political movement follows the ideas of Karl Marx?	*Communism*
8		Which is the adverb in this sentence: *The red ball rolled slowly down the hill*?	*Slowly*
9		Which scale of map would show more detail – 1:500 or 1:50,000?	*1:500*
10		What do Monaco, Brands Hatch and Monza have in common?	*They are all Grand Prix race tracks*
11		Pollution mainly from what causes acid rain?	*Vehicles, factories and power stations*
12		What was another name for the high-wheeled bicycle?	*Penny-farthing*
13		What is a zucchini?	*A courgette*
14		What is a rhombus?	*A parallelogram with equal sides*
15		Which book has sold more copies than any other?	*The Bible (over 2.5 billion)*

Quiz 125
Question 14

Quiz 125
Question 13

Quiz 127 Level 4

Questions

Answers

1. If you are kept apart from other people because you have an infectious disease what are you in? — *Quarantine*

2. What is the main language spoken in Milan? — *Italian*

3. What do bees, ants and nettles have in common? — *They all use acids to defend themselves*

4. What is the liquid in a car battery? — *Weak sulphuric acid*

5. Where is the river Darling? — *Australia*

Quiz 128 Question 8

6. What is the difference between *flammable* and *inflammable*? — *There is no difference in meaning*

7. Which archbishop was murdered in Canterbury Cathedral? — *Thomas à Becket*

8. What is 80.6 divided by 10? — *8.06*

9. What does a philatelist do? — *Collects postage stamps*

10. Who was the first person to fly the English Channel? — *Louis Blériot*

11. What fruit gets its name from Tangiers? — *The tangerine*

12. In which city was John F. Kennedy assassinated? — *Dallas, Texas*

13. How do crocodiles carry their young? — *In their mouth*

14. What is the Milky Way? — *The name of our galaxy*

15. *What you do not wish done to yourself, do not do to others.* Which Chinese philosopher said that? — *Confucius (551BC-479BC)*

Quiz 128 Question 10

Quiz 128 Question 13

Quiz 128 Level 4

Questions

Answers

#	Question	Answer
1	Which famous artist spent four years painting the ceiling of the Sistine Chapel in Rome?	*Michelangelo*
2	*Biannual* means twice yearly. What is *biennial*?	*Every two years*
3	What happens to air if it is compressed and cooled to −200 degrees Celsius?	*It changes to liquid*
4	How many strings does a Spanish guitar usually have?	*6*
5	What language is spoken in Austria?	*German*
6	In sunlight, plants take in carbon dioxide. What do they give out?	*Oxygen*
7	What fictional character went around the world in 80 days?	*Phileas Fogg*
8	It has a quill, barbs and barbules. What is it?	*A feather*
9	Homer's *Iliad* tells the siege of which city?	*Troy*
10	Who wrote *Nicholas Nickleby*?	*Charles Dickens*
11	Which instrument measures the intensity of earthquakes?	*A seismograph*
12	Which unit express the purity of gold?	*The carat*
13	Eating them helps you see in the dark. What are they?	*Carrots*
14	What kind of vehicles first carried people into the air?	*Hot-air balloons*
15	Of which Australian state is Brisbane the capital?	*Queensland*

Quiz 127
Question 15

Quiz 127
Question 11

Quiz 129 Level 4

Questions / Answers

#	Question	Answer
1	Which grain is used to make malt for brewing beer?	*Barley*
2	What are bricks made from?	*Heat-hardened clay*
3	What is the capital of Bulgaria?	*Sofia*
4	The Byzantine empire was part of which empire?	*The Roman empire*
5	What is calligraphy?	*The art of hand-writing*
6	What are soot, charcoal and diamonds made of?	*Carbon*
7	How does a chameleon catch insects?	*It shoots out its very long tongue*
8	Which plant is considered lucky, especially in Ireland?	*The four-leaved clover*
9	Which fuel is found in seams?	*Coal*
10	Which reptiles have fangs?	*Snakes*
11	What was the open square in the centre of ancient Roman cities called?	*The forum*
12	What does *a miss is as good as a mile* mean?	*A small failure is as bad as a big failure*
13	Sugar, bread and potatoes all belong to which food group?	*Carbohydrates*
14	In which year was the Great Fire of London?	*1666*
15	How many sides has a decagon?	*10*

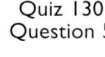

Quiz 130
Question 5

Quiz 130
Question 15

Quiz 130 Level 4

Questions

Answers

		Questions	Answers
1		What do you get if you mix copper and tin?	*Bronze*
2		What did Benjamin Britten do?	*He composed music*
3		What makes the fizz in fizzy drinks?	*Carbon dioxide*
4		What is the capital of New Zealand?	*Wellington*
5		Which bird's nest is called an eyrie?	*The eagle's*
6		What are underground burial places with passages and crypts called?	*Catacombs*
7		How is reinforced concrete different from ordinary concrete?	*It has built-in steel rods for strength*
8		Which insect gives off a yellowish-green light in the dark?	*The firefly*
9		What does *hide your light under a bushel* mean?	*To be modest*
10		Which US statesman signed the Declaration of Independence and invented bifocal glasses?	*Benjamin Franklin*
11		What kind of plant has no roots, stem or leaves?	*A fungus*
12		Blowing, casting and floating are different ways of making what?	*Glass*
13		In *Tom's Midnight Garden*, who was Tom's friend from another age?	*Hetty*
14		What did the Boston Tea Party begin?	*The American War of Independence*
15		What is a portable disk for storing computer information called?	*A floppy disk*

Quiz 129
Question 8

Quiz 129
Question 7

Quiz 129
Question 10

Quiz 131 Level 4

Questions

Answers

		Questions	Answers
1		Which is the largest city in India?	*Calcutta*
2		Which poisonous gas is present in car exhaust fumes?	*Carbon monoxide*
3		In Greek myths which creature had the arms and head of a man and the body of a horse?	*A centaur*
4		If we say someone is *a chip off the old block* what do we mean?	*They are like their father or mother*
5		What is a huge number of fish called?	*A shoal*
6		Which is the largest of the Great Lakes?	*Lake Superior*
7		Which European royal family were for a long time emperors of the Holy Roman empire?	*The Hapsburgs*
8		What kind of animal is a saluki?	*A dog*
9		Who invented the electric motor and the electric generator?	*Michael Faraday*
10		Which two colours are in a rainbow as well as red, orange, yellow, green and blue?	*Indigo and violet*
11		What is the difference between *prior* and *priory*?	*Prior means earlier; priory is a nunnery*
12		Which Indian tribe wiped out General Custer and his men in the Battle of Little Bighorn?	*The Sioux*
13		Which precious metal is used in photography?	*Silver*
14		Who was Salvador Dali?	*A Surrealist painter*
15		Where is your thyroid gland?	*In your neck*

Quiz 132
Question 10

Quiz 132 Level 4

	Questions	Answers
1	Which English doctor discovered how the blood circulates?	*William Harvey*
2	In Greek legend, which woman ran away with Paris, so starting the Trojan War?	*Helen of Troy*
3	Horses' hoofs, birds' beaks and our nails are all made of what?	*Horn*
4	What is another name for a hurricane?	*A cyclone*
5	Which Jewish girl kept a diary about the time her family hid from the Nazis in Holland?	*Anne Frank*
6	What is the capital of Norway?	*Oslo*
7	Which planet has a Great Red Spot?	*Jupiter*
8	What are the larvae of flies called?	*Maggots*
9	Which British general defeated Napoleon at the Battle of Waterloo?	*The Duke of Wellington*
10	Which army left a wooden horse outside the city of Troy?	*The Greeks*
11	Whose grandson was Kublai Khan?	*Genghis Khan*
12	Nutritionally what are the three main kinds of food?	*Carbohydrates, fats and proteins*
13	How many players are there in a rugby league team?	*13*
14	What is the square root of 64?	*8*
15	What does *ephemeral* mean?	*Lasting only a short time*

Quiz 131
Question 8

Quiz 131
Question 3

Quiz 133 Level 4

Questions

Answers

1	?	Which mythical bird burnt itself to death and was reborn from its own ashes?	*The phoenix*
2	📙	What is phonetics the study of?	*Languages*
3	⚛	Which chemical was once used to make matches?	*Phosphorus*
4	⚛	What do doctors give only on prescription?	*Drugs and medicine*
5	🌍	In Holland, what are polders?	*Rich farmland reclaimed from the sea*
6	🌍	Which Australian state has most people?	*New South Wales*
7	⚛	Most of the air we breathe is made of one gas. What is it?	*Nitrogen*
8	?	How many reeds does an oboe have?	*2*
9	🍃	What do you call an animal or plant that gets its food from another living animal or plant?	*A parasite*
10	?	The Russian doctor Ivan Pavlov is best known for his experiments on which animal?	*The dog*
11	📙	What does it mean if someone is *hoist with his own petard*?	*He is caught in his own trap for others*
12	🏛	Who led the Chinese to defeat the Nationalists and establish the Communist Chinese Republic?	*Mao Zedong (Mao Tse-tung)*
13	🍃	Which plant produces marijuana?	*The hemp plant*
14	🏛	Which communist leader wrote *Das Kapital*?	*Karl Marx*
15	🌍	What is a geographic meridian?	*Any line of longitude*

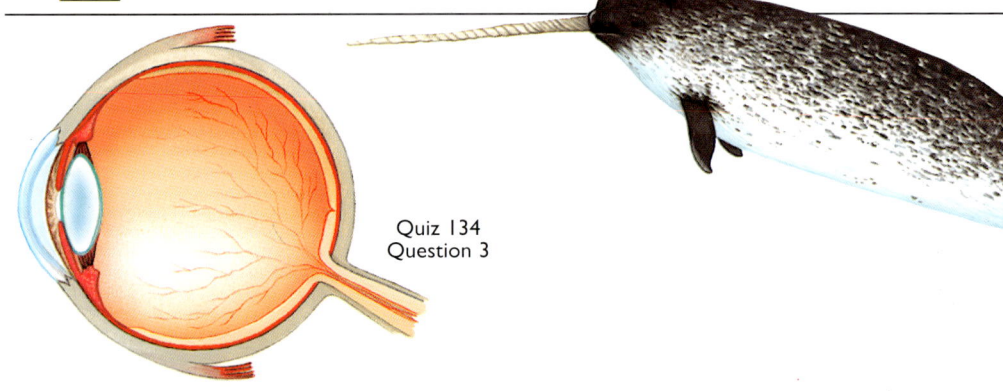

Quiz 134
Question 3

Quiz 134
Question 4

Quiz 134 Level 4

Questions

Answers

#	Question	Answer
1	What is the Greek currency?	*The drachma*
2	What is a gun's calibre?	*The measurement of the barrel diameter*
3	Which part of the body is affected by glaucoma?	*The eye*
4	Which small whale has a twisted tusk?	*The narwhal*
5	Which French king was called the *Sun King* and built the palace of Versailles?	*Louis XIV*
6	Calculate: 0.3 x 0.3	*0.09*
7	Who first used vaccination to protect against infection?	*Edward Jenner*
8	What is the capital of Jordan?	*Amman*
9	What do painters Monet, Degas, and Renoir have in common?	*They were all Impressionists*
10	During which war did the Battles of Agincourt, Crecy, and Poitiers take place?	*The Hundred Years' War*
11	What is the word for the study of heat?	*Thermodynamics*
12	In which century was the Taj Mahal built?	*The seventeenth*
13	What does the disease leukemia affect?	*The blood*
14	What did the storming of the Bastille in 1789 begin?	*The French Revolution*
15	What was Dr Who's time-machine called?	*The Tardis*

Quiz 133
Question 14

Quiz 133
Question 1

Quiz 135 Level 4

Questions

Answers

		Question	Answer
1		Which lines drawn on weather maps show places of equal atmospheric pressure?	*Isobars*
2		What is the Russian national drink?	*Vodka*
3		Hanoi is the capital of which country?	*Vietnam*
4		What does a verb do?	*It describes actions and states*
5		The first Tudor monarch was Henry VII, who was the last?	*Elizabeth I*
6		What is a turbine?	*A wheel turned by flowing liquid or gas*
7		What is another name for a tidal wave?	*A tsunami*
8		Which Australian folk hero was an outlaw and a bank robber?	*Ned Kelly*
9		Which state in the US is known as the Empire State?	*New York*
10		Was Stonehenge built about 10,000, 5,000 or 1,000 years ago?	*About 5,000 years ago*
11		What is an odyssey?	*A long journey or a story of one*
12		On which rock are the Barbary apes found?	*Gibraltar*
13		Which pain-relieving drug is obtained from the opium poppy?	*Morphine*
14		What is millet?	*A cereal crop in parts of Africa and Asia*
15		Who kept a diary of events which included the Great Fire of London?	*Samuel Pepys*

Quiz 136
Question 1

Quiz 136
Question 8

Quiz 136
Question 10

Quiz 136 Level 4

Questions

Answers

1	Which race is named after a soldier's run to Athens in 490BC to bring news of a Greek victory?	*The marathon race*
2	What is the name given to oils and greases?	*Lubricants*
3	Managua is the capital of which Central American country?	*Nicaragua*
4	Radio waves, X-rays, light rays, ultraviolet rays, and infrared rays all have one name. What is it?	*Electromagnetic waves*
5	What does a psychiatrist do?	*Deals with mental disorders*
6	What is 28.6 x 100?	*2,860*
7	Which insect builds rock-hard mounds that can be 6 metres high?	*Termites*
8	Where is your larynx?	*In your throat*
9	Which organization was founded by Sir Robert Peel?	*The British police*
10	How many tentacles has a squid got?	*10*
11	What is the currency of Portugal?	*The escudo*
12	Which Austrian monk discovered the laws of heredity?	*Gregor Mendel*
13	Which word describes a person who reads a lot, and a small insect that eats holes in books?	*A bookworm*
14	What is the capital of Ethiopia?	*Addis Ababa*
15	Who disguised himself as a woman to escape from the English to the island of Skye?	*Bonnie Prince Charlie*

Quiz 135
Question 8

Quiz 135
Question 10

Quiz 137 Level 4

Questions

Answers

#		Question	Answer
1		What are sunspots?	Cooler areas on the Sun that appear dark
2		Which is Europe's busiest port?	Rotterdam in the Netherlands
3		What is the scientific name for a combination of substances that can be separated from each other?	A mixture
4		Which is the highest mountain in North America?	Mount McKinley in Alaska
5		Who was the father of psychoanalysis?	Sigmund Freud (1856-1939)
6		Who fought the Punic Wars?	Rome and Carthage
7		The Parthenon in Athens was dedicated to which goddess?	Athena
8		What is the difference between a tortoise and a turtle?	A tortoise lives on land, the turtle at sea
9		What does a transformer do?	Changes electricity to another voltage
10		Where did the Phoenicians live?	On the coastal lands of the Lebanon
11		What is Thomas Chippendale (1718-79) famous for?	Furniture
12		Which English king spent most of his reign on Crusades in the Holy Land?	Richard I
13		What did John McAdam invent?	A mixture used for road surfaces
14		What are narcotics?	Poisons
15		What was Beijing formerly called?	Peking

Quiz 138
Question 6

Quiz 138
Question 1

Quiz 138 Level 4

Questions

Answers

1	Which is the third nearest planet to the Sun?	*Earth*
2	What does to be *at cross purposes* mean?	*To misunderstand another's intentions*
3	Which early Greek-Egyptian scientist believed that the Earth was the centre of the universe?	*Ptolemy*
4	Which small country nestles in the Pyrenees between France and Spain?	*Andorra*
5	What was the Reformation a revolt against?	*The Roman Catholic Church*
6	What is the name for the bending of light as it passes from one medium into another?	*Refraction*
7	Which disease causes bent legs and is caused by a lack of vitamin D?	*Rickets*
8	Igneous, sedimentary, and metamorphic are all types of what?	*Rock*
9	Who was the first Roman emperor?	*Augustus*
10	What is made from a type of crocus to give a yellow powder used in food flavouring?	*Saffron*
11	Which tropical habitat consists of grassland and scattered trees?	*Savanna*
12	Which UK countries were united in 1707?	*Scotland, England and Wales*
13	The silkworm feeds only on one type of tree. What is it?	*The mulberry*
14	Which vegetable comes in globe and Jerusalem varieties?	*The artichoke*
15	What was Red Rum?	*A race horse*

Quiz 137
Question 5

Quiz 137
Question 11

Quiz 139 Level 4

Questions

Answers

1. Who was the first American to orbit the Earth?

   John Glenn in 1962

2. How do Americans spell *odour*?

   Odor

3. What word means both a race track and a series of lessons?

   Course

4. What do Epstein, Hepworth and Moore have in common?

   They are all sculptors

5. Which large bird of prey has a bare head and neck?

   The vulture

6. In which of Shakespeare's plays does Puck appear?

   'A Midsummer Night's Dream'

7. What are women called who are given a rank similar to a knighthood?

   Dames

8. Cote d'Ivoire is a country in Africa. What is Cote d'Ivoire French for?

   Ivory Coast, the country's old name

9. What is a fresco?

   A painting made on new, still-wet plaster

   Quiz 140 Question 14

10. Who wrote *Auld Lang Syne*?

    Robert Burns

11. What is the old name for Iran?

    Persia

12. Who invented the lightning rod?

    Benjamin Franklin

13. In which country is the port of Alexandria?

    Egypt

14. What type of animal is a samoyed?

    A dog

15. What is the name for an angle between 90 and 180 degrees?

    An obtuse angle

Quiz 140 Question 10

Quiz 140 Question 9

Quiz 140 Question 15

Quiz 140 Level 4

Questions

Answers

#	Question	Answer
1	What was Louisa May Alcott's most famous book?	*Little Women*
2	After which saint is a revolving firework named?	*St Catherine*
3	Who was the reigning British monarch during World War I?	*George V*
4	Which heavenly bodies appear in the sky at regular, but long, intervals and have a tail?	*Comets*
5	What make-up is French for *red*?	*Rouge*
6	Shakespeare wrote a play about two gentlemen. Which city did they come from?	*Verona*
7	Which stimulant is found in coffee and tea?	*Caffeine*
8	Which language is spoken in Brazil?	*Portuguese*
9	Which breed of dog was known as a coach dog?	*The dalmatian*
10	Morello is a type of what?	*Cherry*
11	What do you call a line from the centre of a circle to its circumference?	*The radius*
12	Of which country is Mombasa the chief port?	*Kenya*
13	Against whom did both Samson and David fight?	*The Philistines*
14	What is a cassowary?	*A large Australian flightless bird*
15	What sea animal is named after a flower?	*Sea anemone*

Quiz 139
Question 14

Quiz 139
Question 5

Quiz 141 Level 4

Questions

Answers

#	Question	Answer
1	Which legendary Greek king unintentionally killed his father and married his mother?	*Oedipus*
2	What do ohms measure?	*The resistance of an electrical circuit*
3	Which famous German writer wrote *Faust*?	*Goethe*
4	What is the capital of Jamaica?	*Kingston*
5	What war did the Sopwith Camel fly in?	*World War I*
6	What is the lightest substance?	*Hydrogen (14 times lighter than air)*
7	What do hypochondriacs fear?	*They fear becoming ill*
8	Which ancient Greek is called the *father of medicine*?	*Hippocrates*
9	What was the Holy Grail?	*The cup Christ used at the Last Supper*
10	A study of the animals on which islands helped Darwin to arrive at his theory of evolution?	*The Galapagos Islands*
11	What is the capital of Ontario, Canada?	*Toronto*
12	Which Greek mathematician started modern geometry?	*Pythagoras*
13	What happens when you travel from east to west across the dateline?	*You lose a day*
14	What do fungi lack which most plants have?	*Chlorophyll*
15	Who wrote the book called *Mein Kampf*?	*Adolf Hitler*

Quiz 142
Question 5

Quiz 142
Question 6

Quiz 142 Level 4

Questions

Answers

		Question	Answer
1		If you have an accident, where is it most likely to occur?	*In the home*
2		Who or what killed Cleopatra?	*An asp*
3		What is performed at Glyndebourne?	*Opera*
4		What is curious about the words *abstemiously* and *facetiously*?	*All 5 vowels appear in alphabetical order*
5		Which king married Wallis Simpson?	*Edward VIII*
6		Which is the only marsupial native to North America?	*The opossum*
7		Where did white water racing originate?	*Austria and Germany in the 1930's*
8		What is the outer layer of skin called?	*The epidermis*
9		What is the white trail behind a jet plane composed of?	*Ice crystals*
10		To which island was Napoleon first exiled?	*Elba*
11		Who is Quasimodo?	*The hunchback of Notre Dame*
12		Of which African state is Freetown the capital?	*Sierra Leone*
13		Approximately how long does sunlight take to reach the Earth?	*8 minutes*
14		What is the biggest animal in the world?	*The Blue whale*
15		Which small European country is called a principality because it is ruled by a prince?	*Monaco*

Quiz 141
Question 5

Quiz 141
Question 15

Quiz 143 Level 4

Questions

Answers

#	Question	Answer
1	In which sport might a Fosbury Flop be performed?	The high jump
2	Who commanded the Confederate forces during the American Civil War?	Robert E. Lee
3	Who is buried beneath the altar of St Peter's in Rome?	St Peter
4	In which book by Charles Dickens does Bill Sykes appear?	Oliver Twist
5	Which is the largest brass instrument in an orchestra?	The tuba
6	On which plant did Mendel base his experiments into heredity?	The garden pea
7	What colour were the shirts of Mussolini's fascists?	Black
8	On which river is Aswan?	The Nile
9	Which three kings reigned in Britain in 1936?	George V, Edward VIII and George VI
10	Who invented the diesel engine?	Rudolf Diesel
11	What name is given to ploughed land that has remained untilled or unsown for at least a year?	Fallow land
12	Which bird is known for its booming call and lives in reed-beds?	The bittern
13	Where does the president of Russia live?	The Kremlin, Moscow
14	Which island is joined to Wales by the Menai Bridge?	Anglesey
15	What do you call a word that reads the same both ways?	A palindrome

Quiz 144
Question 11

Quiz 144
Question 9

Quiz 144
Question 15

Quiz 144 Level 4

Questions

Answers

#	Question	Answer
1	Which was the chief god of the ancient Romans? His other name was Jove.	*Jupiter*
2	What do we call coating of iron or steel with a thin layer of zinc?	*Galvanizing*
3	Where is El Dorado?	*Nowhere. It is a legendary country*
4	The peacock is a male peafowl. What is the female called?	*A peahen*
5	Which African nation has the biggest population?	*Nigeria*
6	Which planet is closest to Earth?	*Venus*
7	Kuala Lumpur is the capital of which country?	*Malaysia*
8	Which form of writing ridicules a person or group or society in general?	*Satire*
9	Which sea plant can grow to a length of 60 metres or more?	*The seaweed kelp*
10	Who is king of Spain?	*King Carlos I*
11	What are the teeth at the back of the mouth used for grinding called?	*Molars*
12	What decorated coverings were widely used in the Middle Ages to cover walls?	*Tapestries*
13	How much do 1,000 cc of water weigh?	*1 kilogram*
14	Which novel by Cervantes is about an eccentric knight and his servant Sancho Panza?	*Don Quixote*
15	Who is the Science Officer of the *Starship Enterprise*?	*Mr Spock*

Quiz 143
Question 12

Quiz 143
Question 2

Quiz 143
Question 5

Quiz 145 Level 4

Questions

Answers

1. What is the capital of Indonesia? — *Jakarta*

2. Which brass instrument is made from a metal tube up to 5 metres long and coiled in circles? — *The French horn*

3. Which form of government is organized by the people for the benefit of the people? — *Democracy*

4. What is the name for the parts of the world at the Equator where there is often no wind? — *The doldrums*

5. Our tongue detects four basic tastes – sweet, sour, bitter, and what else? — *Salt*

6. Which English king suffered periods of madness? — *George III*

7. What kind of drugs attack germs in the body, but don't attack the body's cells? — *Antibiotics*

8. Which animal lives in Africa, has ears like a donkey, and catches termites with its long tongue? — *The aardvark*

9. John Adams and John Quincy Adams were both what? — *Presidents of the USA*

10. In which sport do you ride the tunnel of a wave? — *Surfing*

11. Where is the pampas? — *Around Buenos Aires in Argentina*

12. What do we call the numbers 2, 3, 5, 7, 11, 13? — *Prime numbers*

13. Where, during World War II, was the Battle of Alamein fought? — *In North Africa*

14. The Colorado beetle is a pest. Which crop does it attack? — *The potato crop*

15. Which planet has the most moons? — *Saturn (at least 18)*

Quiz 146
Question 6

Quiz 146
Question 5

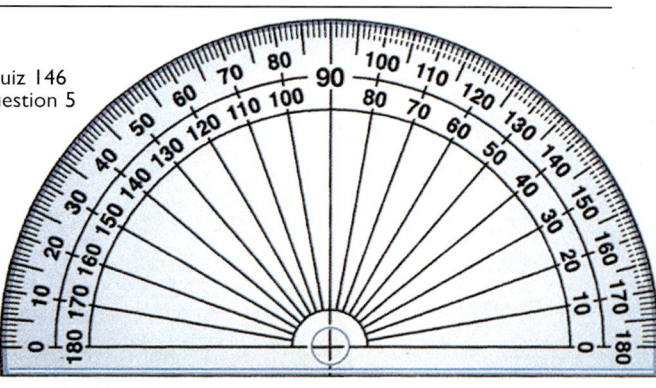

Quiz 146 Level 4

Questions

Answers

		Questions	Answers
1		Where is the Ruhr?	*In west Germany*
2		What kind of wheel turns another wheel to make it go faster or slower?	*A gear wheel*
3		What is the name of the area of the Atlantic Ocean between the West Indies and the Azores?	*The Sargasso Sea*
4		Who invented the sewing machine?	*Isaac Singer*
5		What is an instrument for drawing and measuring angles called?	*A protractor*
6		Dancing the Tarantella was supposed to cure the bite of which spider?	*A tarantula*
7		The buffalo that roamed the American plains was not really a buffalo. What was it?	*It was a bison*
8		In 1085 William the Conqueror made a count of England's land and property. What was it called?	*The Domesday Book*
9		On what does the Earth rely for its oxygen?	*Plant leaves*
10		We know that *catholic* refers to the religion; what is its original meaning?	*All-embracing or broad-minded*
11		Which is the largest country in Africa?	*Sudan*
12		In which war did The Charge of the Light Brigade take place?	*The Crimean War (1854-56)*
13		In 1993, Czechoslovakia split into two separate countries. What are they?	*The Czech Republic and Slovakia*
14		What do you call a word opposite in meaning to another?	*An antonym*
15		What is an element?	*A substance made up of one kind of atoms*

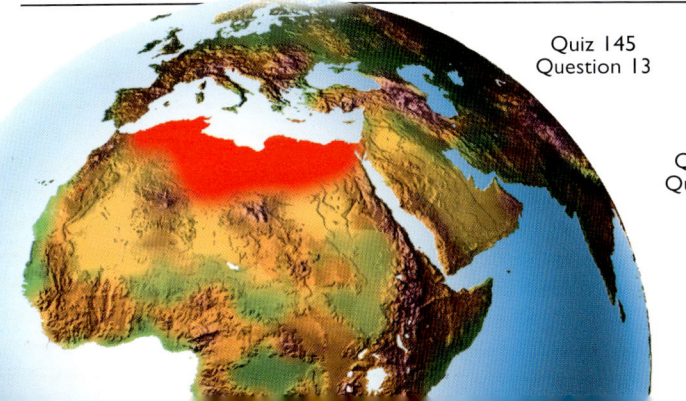

Quiz 145
Question 13

Quiz 145
Question 8

Quiz 147 Level 4

Questions

Answers

		Questions	Answers
1		The Rosetta Stone gave the key to Egyptian hieroglyphics. Where is it?	*In the British Museum*
2		Which of our glands start working at the sight of food?	*Our salivary glands*
3		Riyadh is the capital of which country?	*Saudi Arabia*
4		What is the common name for sodium chloride?	*Common salt*
5		Why is the Dead Sea so called?	*It is so salty no fish can live in it*
6		Which is the largest kind of deer?	*The moose*
7		Who wrote the first great English dictionary?	*Samuel Johnson*
8		What do ferns and mosses have instead of flowers and seeds?	*Spores*
9		Who resigned because of the Watergate Scandal?	*President Richard Nixon*
10		Who were Danton, Robespierre, and Marat?	*Leaders of the French Revolution*
11		Africa's smallest country is on the west coast. What is it?	*The Gambia*
12		In Greek mythology, where did the gods live?	*Mount Olympus*
13		What are skinks, monitors and agamas?	*All types of lizard*
14		What is a herbicide?	*A chemical that kills weeds*
15		The Montgolfier brothers were the first to do what?	*They built the first hot-air balloon*

Quiz 148
Question 10

Quiz 148
Question 14

Quiz 148 Level 4

Questions

1. Sicily has one of the few active volcanoes in Europe. What is it?
2. Which process separates a metal from its ore by heating at a high temperature?
3. In which Shakespeare play does the spirit Ariel appear?
4. Which metal is so soft it can be cut with a knife?
5. Where in South America is the driest place on Earth?
6. What is steel made of?
7. What date was D-Day, when Allied troops landed in Normandy during World War II?
8. Which mother and son were both prime ministers of India?
9. What is the Irish pound called?
10. Which is the largest and heaviest of all snakes?
11. What is a counter-tenor?
12. What type of angle is more than 180 degrees?
13. Against which king was the Gunpowder Plot of 1605 directed?
14. What is the Japanese high speed train known as?
15. What does a geologist do?

Quiz 147
Question 15

Answers

Mount Etna

Smelting

'The Tempest'

Sodium

The Atacama Desert

Iron, with a little carbon

June 6, 1944

Indira and Rajiv Gandhi

The punt

The anaconda (of South America)

A male alto

A reflex angle

James I

The Bullet Train

Studies rocks in the Earth's crust

Quiz 147
Question 13

Quiz 149 Level 4

Questions

Answers

#		Question	Answer
1		Which Greek philosopher was made to commit suicide by drinking hemlock?	*Socrates*
2		The first space traveller was a dog. What was her name?	*Laika*
3		Which is the largest island in the Mediterranean?	*Sicily*
4		Which age followed the Bronze Age?	*The Iron Age*
5		What was the old name for Taiwan?	*Formosa*
6		What is lightning?	*Electricity flowing from cloud to cloud*
7		Which planet was named after the Greek God of the underworld?	*Pluto*
8		Who was the supreme commander of the D-Day landings on June 6, 1944?	*General Eisenhower*
9		What is the study of the body called?	*Anatomy*
10		Which King Louis of France built a great palace at Versailles?	*Louis XIV*
11		Who wrote *Porgy and Bess* and *Rhapsody in Blue*?	*George and Ira Gershwin*
12		What is the Punjab?	*An area of India*
13		With which art movement do we associate Andy Warhol?	*Pop Art*
14		Who wrote *Wuthering Heights*?	*Emily Brontë*
15		What are there lots of between Jupiter and Mars?	*Asteroids*

Quiz 150
Question 5

Quiz 150
Question 13

Quiz 150 Level 4

Questions

Answers

		Questions	Answers
1		What is a family group of monkeys called?	*A troop*
2		What are most grains of sand made of?	*Quartz*
3		What did Martin Luther start?	*The Protestant Reformation*
4		Which planet has the shortest year?	*Mercury (88 days)*
5		Which Russian politician began *glasnost* (openness) and *perestroika* (reconstruction)?	*Mikhail Gorbachev*
6		What is another name for infra-red rays	*Heat rays*
7		Ghana has the largest man-made lake in the world. What is it called?	*Lake Volta*
8		How much liquid would a cube with sides 10 cm long contain?	*One litre*
9		How do male moths find females in the dark?	*By smell*
10		What is Davy Jones's Locker?	*The sea bottom, sailors' graves*
11		Which cud-chewing mammal has a three-chambered stomach?	*The camel*
12		Bangkok is the capital of which country?	*Thailand*
13		What fruit has hands and fingers?	*Bananas*
14		What is the British equivalent of the French *Croix de Guerre* medal?	*The Victoria Cross*
15		What is a transcript?	*A typed or written copy*

Quiz 149
Question 15

Quiz 149
Question 8

Quiz 151 Level 4

Questions

Answers

#	Question	Answer
1	In which city is the Brandenburg Gate?	Berlin
2	Where are red blood cells made?	In the bone marrow
3	Khartoum is the capital of which country?	The Sudan
4	Which element is found in every living thing?	Carbon
5	What did the Romans call London?	Londinium
6	Which abbreviation denotes unknown authorship?	Anon
7	What name did the ancient Greeks give to a supposed large island west of Gibraltar?	Atlantis
8	Where would you find cooling towers?	In power stations
9	Whose mistress was Eva Braun?	Adolf Hitler
10	What is a young female horse less than four years old called?	A filly
11	What form when water evaporates from the Earth?	Clouds
12	What is a *homonym*?	A word with more than one sense
13	Which two American states are not joined to the rest of the states?	Alaska and Hawaii
14	What did Isaiah, Jeremiah and Ezekiel have in common?	They were all prophets
15	What are calamares?	Squid

Quiz 152
Question 8

Quiz 152
Question 1

Quiz 152 Level 4

	Questions	Answers
1	Which member of the camel family has no hump?	*The llama*
2	Which composer wrote the *Brandenburg Concertos*, the *Passions*, and the *B Minor Mass*?	*Johann Sebastian Bach*
3	There are three Baltic States; name two of them.	*Latvia, Estonia and Lithuania*
4	All the colours in paint combine to make black. What do mixing coloured lights give?	*White*
5	What is United Nations Educational, Scientific and Cultural Organization shortened to?	*UNESCO*
6	Which plant leaf can be used to relieve nettle stings?	*The dock plant*
7	Which movements of the sea are called *spring* and *neap*?	*Tides*
8	To which country were convicts transported between 1790 and 1840?	*Australia*
9	What does *Homo sapiens* mean?	*It means thinking man*
10	In which country did the St Bartholomew's Day Massacre take place?	*France*
11	What are young seals and sea lions called?	*Pups*
12	From whom did Winston Churchill take over as prime minister early in World War II?	*Neville Chamberlain*
13	Which two countries do the Himalayas separate?	*India and Tibet (part of China)*
14	What is a lippizaner?	*A type of horse*
15	Who were trapped at Dunkirk during World War II?	*The Allied armies*

Quiz 151
Question 8